Your Affordable
Solar Home

Sierra Club Books

TOOLS FOR TODAY

The economic climate is changing in this country, and a social transformation is occurring too. The resource shortage has caught up with us, and we must find new ways to enhance our lives. But how? Tools for Today are guides for this transitional period. They describe options and suggest strategies that can lead to more self-sufficient living. How to rethink, refurbish, and refit. How to gain access to new systems and human-scale technologies. How to have more in human terms as the times become economically harder. The projects in these books are for the individual, the family, and the community. They're money saving, they're practical, they're ecologically sound, and they look to a bright future.

Books in This Series

The Living Kitchen by Sharon Cadwallader
Your Affordable Solar Home by Dan Hibshman

Sierra Club Books
TOOLS FOR TODAY

Your Affordable Solar Home

by Dan Hibshman
illustrated by Bill Wells

SIERRA CLUB BOOKS
San Francisco

Printed in the United States of America.

A Yolla Bolly Press Book

Your Affordable Solar Home was produced in association with the publisher at The Yolla Bolly Press, Covelo, California. Editorial and design staff: James and Carolyn Robertson, Don Yoder, Diana Fairbanks, Joyca Cunnan, Barbara Youngblood, and Juliana Yoder.

The Sierra Club, founded in 1892 by John Muir, has devoted itself to the study and protection of the earth's scenic and ecological resources — mountains, wetlands, woodlands, wild shores and rivers, deserts and plains. Its publications are part of the nonprofit effort the club carries on as a public trust. There are more than 50 chapters coast to coast, in Canada, Hawaii, and Alaska. For information about how you may participate in the club's programs to enjoy and preserve wilderness and the quality of life, please address inquiries to Sierra Club, 530 Bush Street, San Francisco, California 94108.

Library of Congress Cataloging in Publication Data

Hibshman, Dan, 1945-
Your Affordable Solar Home.
"A Yolla Bolly Press book."
Bibliography: p. 119.
1. Solar houses. 2. Solar heating — Passive systems. I. Title.
T7414.H53   1983   690'.869   82-10747
ISBN 0-87156-327-4

10   9   8   7   6   5   4   3   2

Contents

About This Book

In December 1980, the little city of Cotati, California, sponsored a design contest:

Can the $20,000 House Be Built?

The City Council of the City of Cotati wishes to open a contest to encourage the development of housing designs which offer alternatives to conventional housing types, and will award building space and water and electrical hookups for five different alternative-type housing units. The winners of the contest will have the opportunity to build their models in a cluster suitable for demonstration, and exhibit them for one year. The city will publicize the models and actively encourage further housing development of this type — affordable housing units.

Recognizing the local lack of affordable housing, no different in any particular from the same lack in thousands of other communities, the contest called for designs that could be constructed for less than $20,000. With the cost of land and other nonconstruction costs added, it was estimated that the houses would sell for $35,000 to $40,000 each.

What sort of house would *that* be? The construction industry certainly wasn't turning out units at that cost. Was it possible? For that amount of money, could a house be built that people would *live* in?

Thirty-five entries came in to the City of Cotati. They were reviewed by a panel of judges and six winners were chosen. A house that cost less than $20,000 to build in 1981 was news then and should not be passed over as quickly as most other news. This book presents the winning designs from the Cotati contest — in the context of a growing, nationwide demand for housing that's affordable now. What you'll find in these pages is not so revolutionary that it could place everyone in a home of their own any more than the best ideas of other times could manage that. But the houses that are described here reclaim a crucial opportunity for millions of people who've come to think that that opportunity is beyond their reach.

The book is divided into three parts. Part One includes a short account of why housing in America has become so unaffordable and traces several paths that lead out of this predicament. At least part of the problem of affordability is bound up in the cost of energy. For that reason, the book also incorporates a Solar Primer for Homeowners. This Primer is introduced in Part One, continues throughout Part Two, and concludes in Part Three.

In Part Two, illustrations and written descriptions detail the winners of the Cotati contest. The Solar Primer is integrated with the descriptions here so that readers can grasp fundamentals of solar energy in the context of actual house designs.

Part Three goes beyond the Cotati contest by examining other options available to people who are seeking affordable housing. Some details of the workings of the contest, plus the names and addresses of the contest winners and a bibliography, will be found in the appendix.

Since this book was written before the winning designs could be built, photographs of finished houses and interviews with the occupants of them were not possible. In addition, neither the $20,000 construction budget nor the projected contribution to heating and cooling by passive-solar design could be evaluated in practice. The value of the book is therefore in the value of the houses *as designs*.

My understanding of the problems of housing affordability and the principles of solar energy and building construction was strengthened with the generous help of many people. All of the contest winners supplied very constructive criticism of my chapters on their designs. In addition, I received valuable insights and patient assistance from Larry Bazzany, John Pateros, Gerald Turner, Duane Hill, Bill Schrage, Robert Schaeffer, Gigi Coe, Eve O'Rourke, James Robertson, Barbara Youngblood, and Nan Trichler. To all of them go my sincere thanks.

Part One
Before Design

Chapter One
A Solar Primer for Homeowners: Beginning

Anyone seriously considering the designs and ideas in this book with a mind to applying them in one's own situation has to grasp some scientific principles. It is worth noting that, despite our society's dependence on technological advance, millions of us have very little idea how things really work. Perversely, this ignorance becomes in many people a point of pride, a way perhaps of blocking out the threat that the complexity and immensity of high technology pose to their self-esteem. Others have blocks against absorbing any and all mathematical, scientific, and technical information — blocks stemming from their school days and unchallenged by their adult careers and interests.

These observations may seem beside the point of this discussion, but taking advantage of the opportunity demonstrated by the Cotati contest calls for a certain set of mind, not just a certain financial outlook. People who cannot understand these houses will not want to live in them and will not know what they're missing as they go on pursuing the unaffordable house. Perhaps the most dangerous effect of the easy living that home technology has delivered in our time is the common assumption that one doesn't need to understand that technology, only enjoy it. Stripped of working knowledge of natural principles, convinced that artificial systems are running smoothly in the hands of experts, the average person is denied a personal sense of universal creation as it sustains daily life — and is therefore vulnerable to the global forces which control high technology.

The Cotati contest strongly suggested that the houses employ passive-solar designs and devices. "Passive" systems are contrasted with "active" systems; while these two terms stake out the opposite ends of the range of possibilities, it's important to note that they are differing means of accomplishing the same things. The fundamental operations that both can perform are heating the house, cooling the house, and heating water for domestic use.

To heat a house, a solar design must provide ways not only to collect energy from the sun but also to store it for use at night and during cloudy periods. To the extent that the design cannot admit or retain sufficient heat when the sun is not shining, the house requires a backup heating system. Since no winning design in the Cotati contest claims to supply 100 percent of the house's need for heat by solar means, each has a backup system.

Active-solar systems employ mechanical devices to move heat from areas of collection to areas of storage and use. Air heated in a collector, for example, is pushed or pulled by a fan. Other types of collectors use water as the medium through which heat is transported; an active system of this type includes a pump to move heated water into storage. Similarly, active systems employ fans, pumps, and other mechanisms to move heat into the living areas of the house where it is finally used. Active systems may involve other devices such as thermostats, switches, valves, and sensors too.

Passive systems work without these mechanical devices. Relying on natural principles that can be used to predict the behavior of light, heat, air, water, glass, concrete, brick, and other building materials, passive-solar design uses the physical structure of the house itself, rather than devices added to that structure, to accomplish the task of heating and cooling. The kind of windows, walls, foundation, floors, and roof; the layout of rooms in a floor plan; the directional orientation of the house on a specific site—these elements, which must be designed into every house, are in a passive-solar design major contributors to heating and cooling. The most significant reason why passive systems make sense economically is that most passive designs are inherently durable. They are intended to last as long as the rest of the house because they *are* the house.

Most solar designs are hybrid systems; that is, they are a mixture of active and passive concepts and materials. Since most of the Cotati winners call for at least one "active" element, they are hybrids. And active-solar houses exhibit design features—having most windows face south, for example—that are not mechanical; they are hybrids too. The simplicity suggested by the definition of passive-solar design is for the most part an ideal, a design goal. The realities of actual construction and specific climate impose limitations on reaching that goal.

The relative simplicity of the Cotati hybrids and similar designs makes passive solar a technology that can be grasped, used, and enjoyed by masses of people. The natural principles behind it are, if pursued to their scientific depths, as mysterious as the cosmos itself; but on this level of practical application, they are straightforward, complete, and very understandable. In fact, most passive-solar theory is part of present-day common knowledge: heat rises.

Heating water and cooling the house are no different as far as basic definition is concerned. They do, however, tie the discussion to the question of needs. Heating the house is a facet of shelter; our need to be out of the elements is largely a biological need to be warm enough. But the need for hot water is not quite so primal and, while no one argues against having it, there is a legitimate debate about the necessary size of storage tanks and the need for hot water to be available on demand twenty-four hours a day.

Cooling, specifically the need for air conditioning, is much more debatable. Low-cost, passive-solar designs cool houses by natural ventilation according to the same principles that heat them. As a step toward the goals of conserving energy and cutting utility costs, air conditioning is something to eliminate if possible. The convenience of the modern cooling system is so impressive that eliminating it sounds like heresy. Nevertheless, while there's no need to condemn air conditioners, people should at least keep in mind that in most places in North America there are ways to do comfortably without them.

Passive cooling is not a foolproof system. "Hot" may be a relative term, but it does describe a real sensation and it's not what you want the inside of your house to be. Still, mechanical devices far simpler and cheaper than air conditioners can add much to the cooling efficiency of the affordable house. Portable fans create breezes and moving air where you want them. Built-in fans do the job of pulling hot air up and away, and they do it from the ideal location: above. At a certain point on many a summer day, the most comfortable place to be is outside. By late afternoon, the north and east sides of the house are in shade and probably receiving more natural ventilation than the house can possibly admit (in most areas of the United States). The pleasing light of late afternoon and evening draws many people out just to enjoy it.

There is no point in denying that a few days each year are just too much. On such days, air conditioners seem an unmixed blessing. But is it worth building one in just for those days? The Cotati houses say, politely, no. Take a siesta or a cold shower; say "Hot enough for ya?" to everyone you meet; or curse and moan and be miserable— just keep in mind that the sun does go down every night.

This may seem naive. But it is necessary to note the costs as well as the benefits of those things we've so quickly come to rely on to guarantee comfort. If the costs aren't too high, then by all means build in the conveniences. If costs are too high, you ought to know that you *can* get along without them.

The part of the country you live in will naturally influence your attitude toward air conditioning, too. There are not that many units in Maine. People in Tucson and El Paso, on the other hand, aren't having to deal with just "a few" very hot days. And the humidity of much of the East and South certainly plays as big a role in summer comfort as the heat.

Each region, though, is the inheritor of traditional designs and strategies that are capable of coping with these conditions. The adobe house of the Southwest, for example, has insulating qualities that give it remarkable cooling capacity. It is a corollary principle of passive-solar design that regional, climate-based architecture is superior to uniform distribution of a few standard models of design over the entire country.

Not only are the principles of using solar energy not new, but solar devices in fact appeared much earlier in this century. In Southern California in the 1920s, there were thousands of rooftop solar water heaters. In South Florida some 15,000 simple solar water heaters were installed between 1945 and 1960, mostly without backup systems. This was when the local cost of electricity was high and other sources of energy were not available; when natural gas became available, these solar systems were no longer of commercial interest.

Passive-solar design is not an exotic technology whose perfection must be awaited. While it is at this time apparently locked in competition with complex modern technologies, it is in fact a practical application of phenomena as old as the earth. For the longest imaginable future, solar is the lifeline on which we can depend. And if our own interest in the future extends to any time beyond the next year or so, then the time to reach for that lifeline is now.

Chapter Two
Choosing Smaller Houses

The key to building a 1980s house for $20,000 is to keep it simple and make it small. The obviousness of this advice, however, obscures a large body of thought and experience and contemporary history that needs to be explored. With the opportunities presented by the simple, small house go a set of personal costs that anyone considering owning one should be prepared to pay. For some, these costs are exorbitant. For others, they are literally nothing. For most people, judging from current standards, these costs can be met through self-examination, adaptability, and an honest appraisal of how you want to live your life.

WHY HOUSES AREN'T AFFORDABLE

A general survey of the reasons why housing is so expensive at present will reveal some familiar causes and a few that aren't so obvious. (Most of the statistical and legal references in this book are to California. Not only was this material easily accessible, but it was also judged to be significant in itself. Some of these statistics may not describe conditions in states that are losing population, but the numbers from California certainly indicate trends in areas where rapid growth is a current phenomenon. In any case, the need for smaller houses and passive-solar designs is nationwide.)

In 1970, about half the American people could afford to buy the average new house; by 1980, this figure had dwindled to 13 percent.

According to *California Journal*, only those Californians with income in the top 15 percent can afford to buy a new single-family house, the average price for which, in the summer of 1981, was $116,000. The monthly payment on a typical thirty-year mortgage was $165 in 1970 in the state; in 1980, it was $844.

Residential land costs in California rose about 400 percent during the seventies. Construction costs rose about 80 percent.

More than 80 percent of those Californians who presently own a home could not afford now to buy the house they're living in.

Government regulation (or overregulation) is the housing industry's primary explanation for the current dilemma. A housing study in one California county indicated that growth-control regulations accounted for more than 27 percent of the increase in real housing prices during the period 1972 to 1979.

The time it takes government agencies to process plans and issue permits adds costs to new houses. According to the California Association of Realtors, the average lead time for a housing project in the state (from the time the project is proposed to the time finished homes are offered for sale) is two and a half years. During that time, developers pay interest and taxes on the land they are holding; each month of delay reportedly adds 1½ to 2 percent to the final cost.

One of the main burdens the industry feels is the state requirement that builders prepare environmental impact reports on medium and large developments. Another aspect of government influence on housing costs in California is large increases in local permit fees and charges for public services such as sewer and water connections.

At the time of this writing, builders and buyers alike are pointing to extraordinarily high interest rates to explain why few new houses are going up and relatively few houses of any age are being sold. The Federal Reserve Board's policy of making money tight to control inflation affects the housing industry more directly and perhaps more drastically than any other.

Apart from being expensive, loan money has become scarcer. During periods of high interest people take money out of savings accounts and move it into investments with superior yields. The phenomenal growth of money-market funds has been made largely at the expense of lending institutions, particularly savings and loans.

To some extent, the housing industry is not merely another victim of federal monetary policy but a specific target of an even larger effort to shift economic priorities. In a 1980 editorial, *Business Week* suggested:

> The diversion of capital from industry to housing — the primary aim of past government policy — is one of the reasons investment in productive activities has been inadequate. The government should wean the housing industry of continuing government assistance and make it stand on its own feet.

Indeed, recent government policy has put "reindustrialization" and support of the competitive position of large industrial corporations ahead of housing as an economic priority.

If we were talking only about inflation and interest rates, then the discussion probably wouldn't be significantly different from a similar analysis written years ago. The numbers are different — more excruciating now — but the solution would still lie with the market system which makes funds available for borrowing and assigns people to houses more or less according to income level. This system is essentially undiminished; but not just the raw numbers are different at this time. More crucially, changed percentages present a quantitatively and qualitatively different picture. In California between 1975 and 1980 home prices rose over twice as fast as people's income. The cost of energy, too, rose much faster than the high rate of inflation during the period. The cost of crude oil rose more than 500 percent between 1973 and 1980. Such leaps threaten budgets that might remain balanced if all costs and wages were inflating at approximately equal rates.

In particular, energy costs now force the prospective homeowner to look not only at a house's first cost (sale price) but at its long-term operating costs as well. We are, of course, used to computing monthly mortgage payments and projecting these long-term costs over the life of the financing. (With variable interest rates, though, even these costs are not fully predictable.) But not long ago it was customary to identify these payments alone (or rent) as the essential monthly cost of housing and then to add "plus utilities" almost as an afterthought. Monthly utility bills for some people are now as high as their mortgage payments were ten years ago.

One-quarter of monthly income was once the strict rule of thumb for how much should go to pay for housing; the government used it to figure rent subsidies for low-income people. Consumers were ill advised to commit themselves to any more than that. But many financial columnists are now telling people to allow up to a third of their monthly income for house payments, and bureaucrats concede that the old rule of thumb is no longer realistic.

The cost of transportation has long since ceased being pocket money for bus fares or small outlays for cheap gasoline. It's another item on a personal budget that has jumped in its percentage demand for cash. Furthermore, it affects housing: relatively cheap land at the edges of cities is not being developed as rapidly as in the past because living there would make commuting to work too expensive for many people. This keeps the pressure on land closer to city centers and helps explain the tremendous increase in land values there.

The list of necessities whose percentage bites of income are growing — and the sizes of the bites — do not have to grow that much before they converge in a pattern that reduces millions of people to merely surviving. None of this income is "discretionary." The luxury, convenience, and glamor that money *can* buy notwithstanding, increasingly vast numbers of Americans cannot keep up.

Who are the people who will respond to the potential of the Cotati designs? Demographic data offer one of many reasons why the United States needs new directions toward affordable housing. The generation of Americans conceived during the post-World War II baby boom, who packed the country's colleges and universities during the late sixties and seventies, is now the bulk of the market for new houses. In California, the number of people between 25 and 44 increased 23.5 percent during the seventies; it is now 31 percent of the total state population. (Of course, many of these people migrated to California from other states.) This group, a distinct bulge in the statistics, will generate massive changes in each American institution it encounters simply by the weight of its numbers. In the eighties it is the majority of potential new homeowners.

The configuration of households in the nation is another key element in the overall demand for housing. Here the social trends of the last thirty years have come home to roost in patterns that increase the demand for housing beyond what might have been expected from the sheer increase in numbers of people. In 1940, the average household size in the United States was 3.67; in 1960, it was 3.33; in 1980, 2.7 people. Where the nuclear family was the dominant form of household, it is now one of several forms. While this change has been alternatively viewed as social breakdown, narcissism, or liberation, the demographic fact remains that single people, divorced and unmarried people, single heads of households, and independent retired and elderly people constitute a huge segment of society whose household size is only one or two.

Doubling up with other families or finding a roommate has long been a response to high housing costs and is quite common today, especially when it comes to renting expensive city apartments. Likewise, economic pressures hold together many marriages and large households which would otherwise live apart. Nevertheless, what statistics note as a smaller household is for many a deliberate lifestyle embodying personal freedom; these people can be expected to seek housing that will enable them to hold onto that freedom.

One manifestation of the current housing crisis is the reduction in the number of rental units being built. After 1972 rents in California rose twice as fast as they did during the previous decade. Some 46 percent of all tenants paid more than one-fourth of their income for rent, and 25 percent paid more than a third of their income for rent. While income for landlords has increased, it

evidently didn't increase fast enough compared to the gains to be made from buying and selling housing units.

There has been a sharp fall in "starts" on rental housing since the early seventies: at the beginning of that decade, the ratio of construction of single-family to multifamily units was 50/50; now it's 70/30. Condominium conversion too reduces the number of attractive rentals. Low numbers of housing starts of all kinds and the unaffordability of so many existing houses have put severe pressure on rental units. Rents are high and vacancy rates low.

The scarcity of affordable housing, however, in no way undoes the fact that millions would like to and could afford to buy a low-cost small house. Many childless couples have simply postponed the creation of a family; they want to make a beginning now with a small, expandable house. Some single people (and parents) may more easily find a (new) spouse if a home already exists. There are people who realize that they can choose between a luxurious home and economic freedom to travel extensively. A satisfactory compromise for them is a small house, a home base whose low initial and operating costs keep money available for travel. Others have expensive hobbies and avocations — collecting, attending numerous cultural events — which they can maintain by cutting back to fundamentals and living in a very modest house. There are people for whom concern about environmental degradation, opposition to nuclear energy, and awareness of other issues constitute a whole philosophy and a guide to proper living. These people are simply looking for a place to live that is in keeping with what they believe.

The classic reasons for buying a house remain unchanged: building equity in a proven form of investment; freedom to alter, decorate, or expand without a landlord's permission; more privacy, more outdoor space, greater security; a stronger sense of home.

SMALLNESS

The most informal survey of the housing stock of the United States demonstrates that there's nothing new about the small house. During the twenties, and again after World War II, small houses (less than 1,000 square feet) proliferated as sufficient space for families with few or no children. While the wealthiest suburbs and grandest (or formerly grandest) neighborhoods may be almost entirely the domain of medium, big, and enormous houses, there's no demonstrable reverse pattern that puts small houses exclusively in the poorest sections. They are scattered throughout communities, built in every style that ever was.

Square footage has always been a reliable indicator of the cost of a house and the economic status of its inhabitants. Systems of values that were dominant long before there was a United States taught — and still do teach — that the bigger the house, the wealthier the family. This worshipful estimate of bigness is deeply embedded in our national psychology.

But square footage is not only what you get for living in; it's also what you have to *heat*. Many big older houses are becoming dinosaurs in markets that no longer have niches for them. The grandeur of earlier generations, well-built and still standing, is destined to be divided into apartments or torn down.

Under the pressure of economic reality, bigness has yielded significantly in the matter of cars. The big models of not many years ago look oversized now to many of their former owners. The price of gasoline has not only rendered tail fins and exterior frills obsolete; substantive changes in engine size and interior design have produced the compact car, the subcompact, the minicar, and a confusing flood of new models intended to service new tastes.

Because of the analogy it makes with houses, an examination of cars is instructive in this regard. People have made adjustments: they have been willing to sit closer together, accept less room for storage, have less power at their command. Has this been a grudging acceptance? The response has been mixed. There is pride in economy, of course, and pleasure in getting into tight parking spaces. The powerful tradition of sport and racing cars has accustomed us to seeing beauty in the lines of a small car. Yet a featureless little box of a car seems robbed of something essential; it's utilitarian to a fault. Some people need big cars, gasoline prices notwithstanding. Many people believe that a big car is safer. And that element of status

and prestige is by no means gone. "If he can afford to drive that thing, he *must* be loaded!" (What powerful irony there is in the fact that so many used behemoths of yesterday are now the only cars that the least wealthy drivers can afford.)

But there are important ways in which the analogy between cars and houses breaks down. While most cars last from five to ten years, the life of a building may well be more than fifty, and that of the streets and utilities that supply it hundreds of years. And while the entire stock of automobiles could be replaced within ten years if a fundamental change was called for, today's decisions in building design and construction establish patterns — and create houses — that will remain with us for decades.

The alternating responses of car buyers and the auto industry are a fascinating case history in changing values. Big cars were out, were back in, were out again. The lead time required for retooling an assembly line demands that carmakers know well in advance what the public wants and will buy. But that knowledge has simply not been available; exacerbated by government action and inaction and by strong foreign competition, the trends have been skewed and unpredictable. The result has been severe economic damage to the principal industry in the country. In 1981 General Motors Chairman Roger Smith commented, "One of our basic concepts is that people don't want small cars. They want fuel-efficient cars."

This quote is interesting evidence of the present outlook; psychologically, GM's concept appears correct and probably applies to people's attitudes toward houses, too. Yet the underlying assumption is that cars (read houses) can be fuel-efficient and not be small. There's a "we can have it all" mentality that is not much changed from the thinking that produced the huge products of the past. Over the long haul, though, like it or not, that assumption may be rudely proved wrong. Understandably, but perhaps disastrously, the businesses of making and selling cars and houses have not devoted a great deal of attention to the long haul.

It is hard to rebut the popular contention that, in driving a small car or occupying a small house, many Americans are "settling for less," with the note of defeat that implies. The notion of lowering expectations, the contrary ideal of small is beautiful, the paradox that somehow less can be more — all these proposals met a reaction in the seventies that ranged among most Americans from cool to outraged. Those reactions didn't disprove the philosophies though; the latter may have been merely the first notes of a theme that will play more insistently and more convincingly when it is sounded against the prevailing music of the eighties. There is simply no guarantee nor even any logic in the belief that things get better as they get bigger.

It is impossible to unhook considerations of house size and cost from fundamental economic attitudes. The house a person will be satisfied — or happy — to live in *is* the biggest single manifestation of what that person believes about wealth, success, lifestyle, work, class, and other basic aspects of one's place in society. But while it is true enough that who we are is expressed by where we live, it is a fallacy that some one-to-one correspondence exists between the outer shelter and the inner human being.

TOWARD THE ESSENTIAL HOUSE

What does a person want in a house? What does a person *need*? Most people spend most of their time indoors, thus demanding of shelter the sophisticated ability to modify the natural environment. Time and technology have advanced that sophistication and in turn have shaped our expectations, which become lodged in our thinking as new "needs."

Productivity in our advanced industrial society relies upon the finely controlled environment as an aid to getting work done. But the home, although it can be, does not have to be so rigorously controlled. It is in their homes that people can regain choice over the elements of their lives.

Needs direct the elements and layout of a house as well as its existence in the first place. We eat: the kitchen. We sleep: the bedroom. We wash our bodies and dispose of their wastes: the bathroom. We relax, socialize, and entertain: the living room. Meeting these rudimentary needs implies a house of some minimum size, divided into at least these four spaces. Nevertheless, a glance at the history of housing in America and at traditional housing in other cultures teaches that such a solution is hardly mandated by nature. When the fireplace served as both heating and cooking system, there was not inevitably a separate kitchen. In some cultures, bedding is stored during the day and set out at night in a central living space. The outhouse or privy was a separate structure in early housing schemes and therefore did not have to be designed under the same roof as cooking and sleeping areas.

Native building styles that use local materials and respond to local climate — "vernacular architecture" — embody design decisions that are relevant to us. Traditional Japanese houses have open floor plans that can be flexibly rearranged with sliding partitions. Old Mediterranean villages demonstrate clustering that provides each house with solar exposure, natural cooling, and ways of balancing high population density with privacy and individuality. Underground houses — a current hot topic with solar enthusiasts — are the time-tested choice for shelter in certain regions of China.

Technological progress seductively carries with it an aura of moral progress. "Better" indiscriminately suggests more convenient devices and improved human behavior. Thus indoor plumbing and the flush toilet did more than save trips to the outhouse; they cast a stigma on the older ways and elevated the newer one to some variety of righteousness. Creation of consumer demand by advertising utilizes the same principle, though rarely explicitly. "New improved" soaps, "state-of-the-art" stereos, and "the latest" fashions from New York, Paris, and Milan demand that their predecessors be replaced. Advertisements and newspaper and magazine coverage of the latest fashion in housing *create* demand as much as they reflect current taste.

Thus demand for houses is based in large part on what is shown to be available; few consumers can demand what they don't know about or what doesn't exist. The movement toward small houses bears on this problem directly. And it implies that what people require is "enough," not "more." What's needed now are some examples of the kind of house that has been only suggested so far. This, of course, brings us round to the winners of the Cotati contest.

The rules of the contest ensured that the winning designs would be largely conventional. This was, of course, as it should be, since conventional designs could demonstrate applicability in other typical American cities and towns, too.

"Conventional" translates into several specifics — starting points for the designers, facts of life for the occupants. First, the houses all have standard electric hookups: power lines running through the framework, sockets in the walls. This means that in these houses major and minor appliances can all be used as they would in any house. It also means that the occupants rely on the centralized system of electric power generation in the United States and remain subject to the tribulations of that system in its demand for fuel.

Second, the building materials and construction techniques employed in these houses are, with some innovative exceptions, standard. There is no material so exotic that it cannot be found at every supply house, no technique so strange that it isn't known or easily learned by every builder. This means that the houses will look and feel and in fact *be* like nearly all the modern housing we see around us every day. These homes are not unique; they are not even very unusual in appearance. There are no tricks.

Third, the plumbing is standard. All the houses have hot and cold water, showers, toilets. The water comes in from a standard municipal water supply. Waste leaves the house via conventional sewage pipes.

These houses were designed to cost less than $20,000 to build in 1981. By the standards of the day, this cost is shockingly low. But "you get what you pay for" — the first thought of many upon hearing this news — is at best a half truth. It implies that quality lies along a scale that is mirrored *exactly* by cost. A new house can, of course, vary tremendously in quality. There are inferior materials and there are inferior building practices and if these have gone into a house, its quality will surely have been lessened.

But *how* a person lives is a major consideration in the quality of a house because it has a great deal of influence on the design. Let's make the positive (though not entirely warranted) assumption that the house, following the design, is built properly. Materials are used correctly and assembled with a high degree of concern and skill. Where time is required to do a job right, let's assume the time was taken. So we have a house on which the roof doesn't leak, the foundation isn't cracked, and the nails aren't popping out. This is a house that thousands of professional builders, and plenty of owner-builders, are capable of making.

Many readers should consider these designs as core houses — the beginning, that is, of expansion and improvement according to personal tastes and needs. Nearly every homeowner can carry out a serious program of home improvement as well as repair and maintenance. Rather than the fully finished luxury home that they can't afford, millions would be grateful for a less finished start that they can afford.

Upgrading and finishing can obviously be done by hired help and subcontractors, too. If the production of new houses concentrated more on small units, the demand for professional "remodels" and "add-ons" would be strong and long-lived. People's incomes fluctuate, and money for home improvement can likely be managed later on. Houses built from the Cotati designs would be, for millions, a sufficient beginning.

Part Two
Six Affordable Houses

and Solar Primer: Continued

Chapter Three
The Northbay House

Northbay Architects is Phil Davis and Richard Benson. Both are transplants from Southern California, a region where, they believe, many of the current problems of American housing are best exemplified. Extravagance in energy, water, and land use was characteristic in the communities they left behind; conservation by design is the answer they brought north with them to Cotati.

The Northbay house is straightforward and practical. It cuts corners but offers a generous supply of space while accommodating fundamental needs. "Cutting corners" suggests a shortcut, taking a direct line to save distance and time. But cutting (out) corners is quite a literal technique in designing affordable houses. Phil Davis notes that every exterior corner in a plan involves more complex carpentry, which adds time and cost to the finished product. Zigging and zagging walls can create unusual shapes in rooms, often with the pleasure that variety brings. But interior decoration can achieve similar effects at much lower initial cost; furthermore, decor can keep changing, while the shape stays.

Simple geometry shows that the square is the shape with the highest ratio of area to perimeter. When it comes to construction, this academic fact has very practical ramifications. The area (in square feet) of a house is how much room you have to live in. The perimeter (the number of linear feet of wall) is where most of the cost of building is concentrated. The shortest perimeter also tends to present the smallest surface area to the outside,

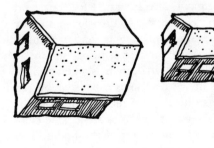

1,000 ◻ House: 126' Perimeter   1,000 ◻ House: 162' Perimeter

The Northbay House

DESIGNER:	Northbay Architects
AREA:	851 square feet plus 171 square feet (loft)
FLOOR PLAN:	two bedrooms plus open loft accessible by ladder
FOUNDATION TYPE:	concrete slab
CONSTRUCTION TYPE:	standard frame, masonry block interior walls
PASSIVE-SOLAR FEATURES:	*space heat:* concrete slab and masonry block walls as thermal mass; *water heat:* breadbox; *other:* recessed entry, openable skylights, roof slope and depth of overhangs calculated for specific site
BACKUP SYSTEMS:	woodburning stove, gas water heater
OTHER FEATURES:	stacked washer/dryer

and this matters because it's the surface area through which most of the heat escapes from inside.

Of course, there are many mitigating factors which pull most houses into rectangles or groups of them. Squares may appear boring, too uniform. Heat loss is much greater through windows than through walls, so the surface area devoted to them is more significant than the total amount of wall. And while the square presents faces of equal length to each of the four directions, an ideal passive-solar design exposes a longer surface to the south than to east or west.

Every design represents the designer's resolution of dozens of apparent conflicts. Compromises among the demands of cost, efficiency, law, and personal taste yield answers to questions posed by differing sites, climates, budgets, and personalities. The Northbay floor plan is nearly square.

This floor plan lends itself to division into quadrants. Mirror-image bedrooms separated by the bathroom make up the two rear quadrants. Entrances to all three of these rooms are located close to each other near the center of the house. The bathroom is actually two compartments separated by a sliding door: in the rear compartment are a shower/bath and toilet; in the forward one a sink and plenty of storage space.

Overhangs, several roof slopes, and the visual variety of glass windows, doors, and skylights effectively counter the boxy basis of the plan outside. Inside, partitions and several wall and floor textures supply a comparable variety. The Northbay plan shows how the principles of passive-solar design in small houses can be accommodated in attractive conventional terms. The house looks "normal," but the elements of its normality are not there merely to conform. They have multiple reasons for being and are coordinated in an integral design.

(At this point we will digress from description of the Northbay house in order to consider more passive-solar fundamentals. The Solar Primer for Homeowners, which began in Chapter One and is an integral part of this and the next six chapters, is presented in this manner so that readers can grasp these fundamentals in the context of actual house designs.)

No matter where its main entrance is located, the solar house faces south — to the source of the energy it is designed to collect. Every solar design concentrates its glazing (windows, doors, and skylights of glass or clear plastic) on this south face, reduces it on the east and west, and all but eliminates it on the north.

This orientation may be common knowledge,

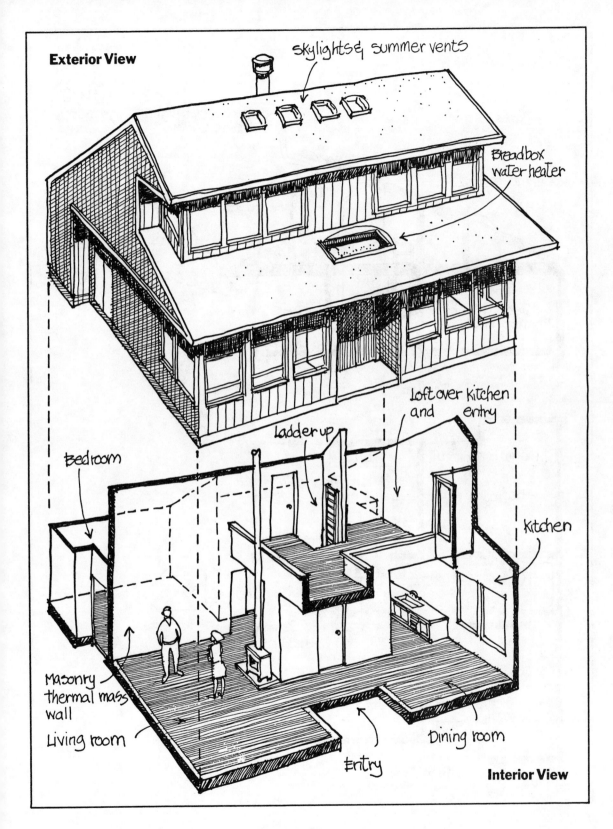

Exterior View

skylights & summer vents

Breadbox water heater

loft over kitchen and entry

ladder up

Bedroom

Kitchen

Masonry thermal mass wall

Living room

Entry

Dining room

Interior View

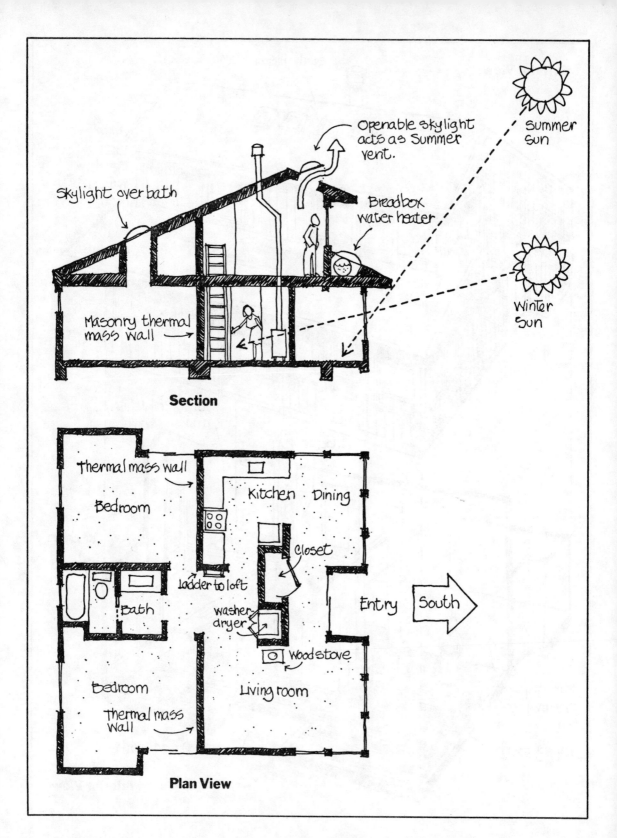

Openable skylight acts as summer vent.

Skylight over bath

Summer Sun

Breadbox water heater

Winter Sun

Masonry thermal mass wall

Section

Thermal mass wall

Bedroom

Kitchen   Dining

Closet

ladder to loft

Bath

washer dryer

Entry   South

Bedroom

Wood stove

Living room

Thermal mass wall

Plan View

but it's well worth reviewing: a good deal of common knowledge is based on shaky foundations. Where *is* the sun? In the northern hemisphere, at midday, it is always south of an east-west line running directly overhead. Thus we can always determine north at noon: by looking at the direction of a shadow. The sun's precise position in the sky at any given time is an expression of the time of day, the time of year, and the orientation of the earth to the sun.

The time of day: no matter what the season, the sun appears to rise and fall along a smooth curve, reaching its high point sometime around midday.

The time of year: the sun follows a longer path in summer than in winter. In winter it rises "south of east" and sets "south of west"; in summer it rises and sets north of the east-west line. The summer path is higher in the sky than the winter path. Summer days are longer. The length of the sun's path is the same on the equinoxes — usually March 21 and September 21.

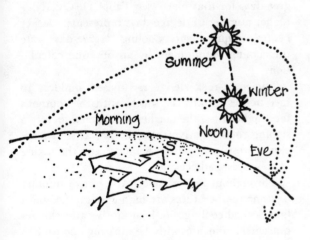

All of this was observed by prehistoric people. But other factors that determine the sun's position were grasped only as people gained a clearer idea of the earth as a body in space.

The earth is a rotating sphere. Result: day and night. The rotation is from west to east. Result: the sun appears to rise in the east and set in the west. A location to the east of you receives first morning light before you do. Result (out of human need): time zones.

The earth revolves around the sun. Result: the seasons. Obvious, yes? But let's examine this one more closely. The explanation of the seasons lies in the combined facts of the earth's revolution around the sun and its tilting on an axis. The tilt (toward Polaris, the North Star) remains nearly constant throughout the year; that is, the planet's axis keeps pointing in the same direction.

But with the earth's movement around the sun, that same tilt puts us in different configurations relative to the sun at different times of the year. Our summer in the northern hemisphere occurs when the tilt is toward the sun. The sun's rays pass through less of earth's atmosphere to reach us then. This lessens the amount of solar radiation absorbed and reflected by the atmosphere; more reaches the earth's surface.

Our winter is when the tilt is away from the sun. This configuration makes winter sunlight pass through more of the atmosphere to reach us. More of its energy is dissipated by the atmosphere, making less of it available to us than in summer.

The earth's atmosphere thus plays a crucial role in determining how much solar energy is available. The amount of this energy falling on any point at the *outer* limits of the atmosphere is constant. (The sun's output of energy is constant, in other words.) But on the surface of the planet, because the atmosphere acts as a filter, the amount varies.

The tops of clouds absorb and reflect sunlight, thus reducing the amount that can reach the ground. But even clear skies are not empty of matter, so they too reduce the amount of solar energy we receive. The blue color of the sky is caused by the absorption/reflection of colorless light by particles of gases, dust, and water vapor in the atmosphere. The colors of sunrise and sunset are created by that light's passage through more of the atmosphere.

The earth itself gradually absorbs and holds heat. This accumulation explains why our hottest weather typically comes in August even though the sun reaches its highest point at the summer solstice, usually June 21. Similarly, the coldest time of year is generally later than the winter solstice because the planet takes several months to cool.

It is *not* true that our summer season is caused by the planet being closer to the sun in the summer months. In fact, the earth is farther from the sun in June than in December. Remember in this connection that seasons are reversed between the earth's hemispheres. It is winter in Chile in July because the sun is lower in the sky then from that vantage point on earth, and solar radiation must pass through more atmosphere to reach the southern hemisphere.

Even without the atmosphere's influence, the sun's lower position in the winter sky causes its radiation to be less concentrated. A flashlight shining on a surface demonstrates the principle. From directly above, the light is concentrated in a circle on the surface; but from any lower position, the light spreads out in larger, more oval shapes. Because it's the same amount of light (energy), when the angle of the source is lower, the amount of light falling on a point on the surface is less concentrated.

Even with these seasonal differences, the intensity of the sun's radiation in winter is great enough to make a major contribution to home space and water heating. Extended periods of cloudiness and the amount of difference between indoor and outdoor temperatures are the problems that must be solved; solar energy is sufficient — with proper design — to solve them an impressive percentage of the time in nearly every location.

A useful measure for comparing the heating requirements of different locations is the unit called degree-days. Using a comfortable indoor tempera-

TABLE 1			
NORMAL TOTAL HEATING DEGREE-DAYS (BASE 65°F)			
Atlanta	2,983	Minneapolis	10,606
Baltimore	4,654	Oakland	2,870
Boston	5,634	Phoenix	1,765
Chicago	6,155	St. Louis	4,900
Dallas	2,363	Seattle	4,424
Denver	6,283		

ture as a base (for example, 65°F) degree-days express the difference between a location's average temperature and the base — that is, the amount the temperature must be raised to achieve comfort. If the average temperature in Chicago on a given day in January is 30°F, then the difference is 35. The sum of the differences for all the days of the heating season is the number of heating degree-days for that place (see Table 1). Clearly, a higher number of degree-days represents a larger heating requirement. Cooling degree-days rate the cooling requirement by an opposite calculation.

Ancient Greek designers advised builders to face houses toward the south, with the southern face higher than the northern and consequently a sloping roof. The Northbay house, as seen from east or west in elevation, demonstrates the taking of this classic advice.

Throughout North America, average summer daytime temperatures are high enough that most homes need cooling, not heating. Because this requirement coincides with the sun's high position in the sky, overhangs and other shading devices can keep its rays from entering a house through glazed surfaces. The shorter section of roof sloping down from the Northbay's peak creates the overhang that will shade its south face in summer. The roof slope and overhang length are calculated by noting the winter and summer angles of the sun on the specific site.

A second benefit of this fundamental design stems from the fact that most of our severest weather blows in frigidly from the north. By turning its back to that wind and giving it the smallest possible surface to attack, the solar house protects itself. The Northbay roof also overhangs a long strip along the east and west walls. This overhang protects side entries and shades those walls during the middle of summer days.

Continuous chemical transformation of hydrogen into helium inside the sun releases energy, which radiates from that star in all directions. The tiny fraction of it which reaches earth is sufficient to support all life on our planet. That energy takes many forms. Energy forms can be understood as

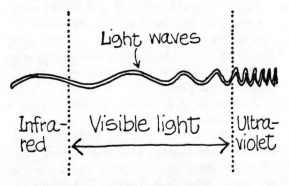

entities of various wavelengths. Visible light occupies a middle portion of the range of energy waves; the visible spectrum runs from the longer waves of red light to the shorter waves of violet light. Beyond violet (ultraviolet) are high-energy radiations such as gamma rays and X rays. Radiations that occur in waves longer than those of red (infrared) include heat, radio, and sound waves. Shorter wavelengths indicate higher levels of energy.

Glass allows visible light and other solar radiation to pass through it with very little absorption or reflection. Entering a house through a window, for example, this energy strikes whatever materials lie in its path. It strikes the dust particles, gas molecules, water vapor, and other ingredients of air in the room. This input of energy causes them to move faster and to spread out. They rise and are replaced by colder, denser air from shaded parts of the room. The solar energy strikes your skin. It makes *your* molecules move faster—you sense this as heat.

Each object responds to being heated according to its unique properties. Heated air spreads and rises; so does heated water. The movement of both these fluids as they are warming or cooling is called *convection*. Neither a metal rod nor a wooden chair visibly spreads out when it's heated, but heat is transmitted from molecule to molecule in response to the same solar input. One material feels hot to the touch, the other merely warm; its molecular structure gives each a characteristic capacity to *conduct* heat—that is, to transfer it through direct contact. Having increased its load of heat, an object also gives off heat by *radiation*. This heat travels away from the object in waves, too, but in infrared waves, which are longer than waves of visible light. The principles of convection, conduction, and radiation are keys to understanding how passive-solar houses work.

Glass happens to allow light waves (shorter) to pass through it much faster than infrared waves (longer) can. In practical terms, this means that the heat produced inside a house cannot escape through glass nearly as fast as light can enter through it. This phenomenon—the "greenhouse effect"—is familiar from the dramatic buildup of heat in a closed car left standing in the sun. Light passes through the car's windows and is absorbed not only by the air in the car but also by the seat, steering wheel, dashboard, and other materials; these reradiate it as heat, which cannot quickly escape back through the glass.

This principle works wonderfully for heating a house, too—while the sun shines. On clear winter days, in fact, the sun provides a large heat surplus. But at night heat inside a space disperses—by

Greenhouse Effect

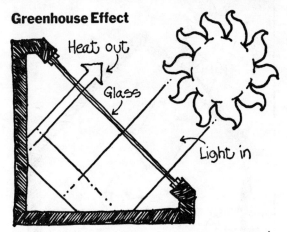

Long light waves bounce around and become short heat waves. Long waves pass through glass well, while short waves don't.

convection, conduction, and radiation — through walls, windows, floor, and roof. Unless the heat is stored in some way during the day, it will be gone not long after the sunlight has stopped entering the space. The second law of thermodynamics is a helpful guide to understanding this process. It states (among other things and here in simple terms) that heat always tends to flow from a warmer body to a colder one. As a system, two objects tend toward equilibrium; the warmer body becomes colder and vice versa.

Clearly, heat *storage* is the key. Unless heat is to be produced continuously, some method must be employed to hold onto it. Continuous production of heat is possible, of course, but only at the cost of continuously burning fuel. One way to hold onto heat is to slow the rate at which it escapes. This is the job of insulation, the thorough use of which is essential in order to make passive-solar designs work efficiently. But heat can also be stored for later use by taking advantage of the heat-storage abilities of certain materials. Brick, concrete, or stone walls and floors can act as an efficient "thermal mass." The material's color, surface, and density and the correct thickness of construction enable a thermal mass to absorb and store solar radiation.

Dark colors absorb more solar energy than light ones. (In fact, a material's color is the visible evidence of how much light energy it is absorbing.) Shiny, smooth surfaces reflect more solar energy than dull, rough ones. Heavy, dense materials absorb more solar energy than light, porous ones. Different materials absorb energy at different speeds, too.

When the source of energy is cut down or out (by clouds or sunset) the thermal mass stops absorbing energy and starts to radiate heat back to the environment around it. The absorption was slow and the radiation is slow, too. This time lag is crucial; the need is for a source of heat long after sunset, and a thermal mass provides it by releasing its stored heat slowly.

The ability of a material to function as a thermal mass is indicated by several measurements. The "specific heat" of a material is expressed as the number of British thermal units (Btus) needed to raise one pound of the material one degree Fahrenheit. The specific heat of water is agreed upon as 1.0; in other words, one Btu is defined as the amount of heat it takes to raise a pound of water one degree Fahrenheit. (One Btu is a small amount of heat — about equal to the heat created by burning one kitchen match.) The

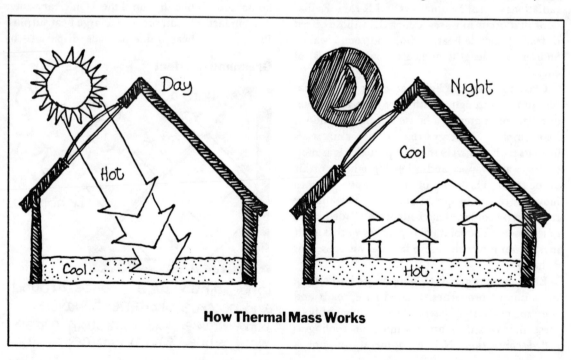

How Thermal Mass Works

TABLE 2
SPECIFIC HEAT OF SOME
COMMON SUBSTANCES

Material	Specific Heat (Btu/lb – °F)
water	1.0
wood (oak)	0.57
air	0.24
brick	0.20
concrete	0.156
steel	0.12

specific heat of some other materials is listed in Table 2. Note that water has the highest specific heat of them all. This means that it takes the most heat to raise its temperature, heat which is being *stored* in the water. The more Btus being stored in a thermal mass, the more heat it can release later.

Water is a liquid; it has to be contained and it has no structural uses (except for houseboats). Some solar designers employ contained water as thermal mass; others look to building materials which can function as thermal mass while, as walls or floors, they support their own weight and that of other parts of the house.

Passive-solar homes can collect and store heat by either direct gain or indirect means. In direct-gain systems, solar radiation enters the living area and is collected and stored right there. In indirect-gain systems, solar radiation is collected and stored outside the living space and then transmitted to the interior. This can be done by passive means or, in the case of a hybrid system, with the use of fans.

Heating the Northbay house is accomplished by a direct-gain system. After entering the house through its south-facing windows, doors, and skylights, the sun's rays then strike a six-inch concrete slab floor. While the specific heat of concrete is less than that of water, concrete is denser than water, as measured in pounds per cubic foot. A cubic foot of concrete weighs more than an equal volume of water. The truly functional measure by which to compare thermal masses is "heat capacity," which is specific heat multiplied by density. It takes more Btus to raise the temperature of a six-inch-thick concrete slab than to heat an equal volume of water — and you can walk on it!

Remember: those Btus are being stored. Does a thermal mass have to be "turned on" to get that heat out of storage? No. The second law of thermodynamics tells us that as soon as the temperature of the air in a room is less than that of the thermal mass, the mass will stop absorbing and start releasing heat. The heat capacity of some other common building materials (Table 3) is impressive, too.

The key issue for a passive-solar house designer to consider is getting sufficient heat absorbed by the thermal mass. Windows and other glazing need to be large enough in area to let in enough solar energy. Thermal masses must be located in a way that maximizes the amount of direct sunlight they receive.

Sunbeams striking Northbay's concrete floor are partially reflected onto a concrete interior wall standing at about the midline of the house. This wall separates the bedrooms and bath from the more frequently used living areas; a sliding door is located at about the middle of it. From the sun's low angle in the winter sky, it will strike the lower portions of this wall directly, allowing it too to function as thermal mass. This portion of the wall is exposed only on the western side; the other half stands behind some of the kitchen counter and appliances. The heat stored in it is later released not only to the living areas but also to the northern half of the house.

Although heat is absorbed by a shaded thermal mass too (the upper part of this midline wall, for

TABLE 3
HEAT CAPACITY OF SOME
COMMON SUBSTANCES

Material	Specific Heat	Density (lb/cu.ft.)	Heat Capacity (Btu/cu.ft. – °F)
water	1.0	62.4	62.4
wood (oak)	0.57	47	26.8
air	0.24	0.075	0.018
brick	0.20	123	25
concrete	0.156	144	22
steel	0.12	489	59

example, and all of this wall at certain times and seasons), four times as much shaded mass is needed to equal the heat capacity of a thermal mass struck directly by the sun. So this wall is secondary to the concrete floor as thermal mass.

A rough rule of thumb suggests that, for direct gain, each square foot of window needs about two cubic feet of concrete, brick, or stone thermal mass. The more a house depends on passive-solar heating and cooling, the more precise the design calculations must be. Many studies have developed data from which precise calculations can be made.

For the moment, consider in general the problems created by incorrect ratios of "glass to mass." When there's too much glass, the house will overheat on a sunny winter day and lose heat more rapidly than it has to. The mass can only absorb heat at a certain fairly slow rate, and surplus will be absorbed more rapidly by the air; heated air can escape quickly, defeating the time-lag storage capability of the mass.

When there's too much mass, it is usually because the mass is too thick. The mass tends to function as a heat sink, continuously absorbing heat in every molecule. But distribution of heat through the mass is uneven, since the deeper parts of the mass heat more slowly. The difficulty of heating all of a too thick mass means that its average temperature will not rise as much as that of a thinner mass, and, in practice, less heat is available for release at night. Even though they weigh the same (and thus have equal heat capacity), a hundred-square-foot wall eight inches thick is more effective than a fifty-square-foot wall sixteen inches thick.

Designs with the right amount of south-facing windows do not have to look too glassy or give up a feeling of indoor privacy; nor must the residents be troubled by glare. While these are potential problems, in most American climates an effective amount of glazing will in fact occupy a moderate percentage of the entire south wall.

Davis and Benson figure that their passive system will supply 60 to 70 percent of the space heating needs of the Northbay house — in January — according to statistics for average temperatures in Cotati. For days of well below average temperature and stretches of cloudy days when the solar contribution decreases, a woodburning stove can supply the heat the house will need.

Advances in the efficiency of woodburning stoves have made these devices entirely reliable heaters. Given the compact floor plan of the Northbay house, there is no question that one of these stoves can adequately warm the entire house. Davis and Benson call for the stove to be standing near the middle of the house, slightly to the south, and backed by a concrete masonry wall. The stove will also radiate heat to this wall, where the heat will likewise be stored for later release. (The time delay would be different in this case since the stove will often be producing heat at night.) The refrigerator is backed on two sides by other legs of this same wall; to perform their cooling function, refrigerators exhaust heat, which can, with this design, be stored in the walls.

The south-side door is deeply recessed from the main line of windows and is thus protected from the elements. In this position, it is as open to the low winter sun as the windows, but even more shaded from the high sun of summer. Inside the sliding glass doors, forty-eight square feet of space is defined as entry — neither living room nor dining room although flowing directly into both. The interior concrete masonry walls referred to in the preceding paragraph block in most of this space and trap much of the cold air that enters whenever the doors open. Such a trap can modify heat loss considerably; imaginatively decorated, it can also become an amenity, a welcoming area that encourages socializing.

An amenity of a more private sort is provision for two sliding glass doors connecting each bedroom directly with the outside. Located on the east and west walls, these doors will also contribute to cooling the house in summer.

Window overhangs are not in themselves enough to cool the house; they merely keep unwanted rays from striking the interior directly. In order to cool the house, ventilation must offer ways for hot air to rise and leave. The "chimney effect" is the common name for this updraft, and intelligent design uses it to vent hot air. By placing intake vents low (near the floor) on the north wall and exit vents high on the south wall, the design ensures that incoming air will be the coolest air available in the vicinity of the house. The location of obstructions such as interior walls is extremely important in this regard; mistakes can leave certain rooms with no possibility of ventilation.

To facilitate ventilation, all the south, east, and west windows of the Northbay house are in two sections, the upper fixed and the lower openable. The sliding doors and the four skylights can be opened too.

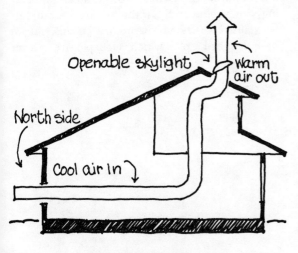

Summer Cooling

To make best use of a thermal mass floor, many passive-solar designs have an open floor plan in which kitchen, dining, and living rooms are not separate but flow into each other. This openness contributes to successful ventilation as well, since the upward flow of warm air can be drawn directly from much of the house.

Landscaping enters the design picture at this point. The right location of the right trees and shrubs makes a substantial difference in cooling a house without mechanical systems. The leaf canopy of deciduous trees to the southeast or southwest can cast summer shade on the house's south face. These same trees, leafless in winter, will not much reduce insolation (amount of solar energy) during the heating season.

Since the most uncomfortable time on a very hot day is the middle to late afternoon, shade trees on the west can help in summer. These can be evergreen; if so, they'll block out westerly winds in every season. The house creates its own shade on the north side, but evergreen trees here will slow down the northerly winds responsible for North America's nastiest winter weather. Enjoyment of morning light and the fact that the beginning of a hot day is likely to be its least oppressive time suggest the advisability of leaving the east side of a house free of trees.

Low-growing shrubs and even grass take part in the cooling plan, too. By covering the ground and, with their dark colors, absorbing light and heat, these plants create a microclimate that is much cooler than that of nearby paved or unplanted zones. Furthermore, they retain more moisture than these other surfaces. If air for ventilation is to be drawn in at a particular location, landscaping of this sort can cool it before it enters the house.

The art of landscape design gains exceptional prominence in the solar age. By knowledgeably selecting among so many available species, its practitioners can not only create shade but even funnel winds to where they are desired. Rules of thumb dictate optimal height and distance from the house to accomplish this. To increasing numbers of people, an edible landscape makes excellent sense. When trees bear fruit or nuts as well as cast shade and divert winds, households are remarkably well served by "mere" plants.

The long slope of the roof creates a large interior space which the Northbay design utilizes as a loft. It is from this loft that all the skylights can be reached — a crucial activity for summer cooling since without the skylights open the chimney effect is largely undone. The loft will look down over railings onto the living and dining areas. To save the space a stairway would require, the only access to the loft is via a fixed vertical ladder. This solution does not conform to the building code's requirements for access to a bedroom, however, so strictly speaking, the loft must be regarded as a storage area only. In practice, though, it will no doubt serve as a great place for kids to play or for adults to retreat. Lofts are remarkably warm in winter.

The ladder climbs a concrete block wall set at a right angle to the midline wall; on the wall's other side, a stacked washer/dryer unit is neatly fitted in. This arrangement is in keeping with the architects' conviction that the problem of affordable housing is one that must be solved above all with young families in mind. This idea also influenced their decision to create separate rooms instead of the cheaper and easier design of one large universal space.

The Northbay house develops hot water in a solar device called a "breadbox" water heater, which is mounted on the roof above the south entry. Several of the Cotati houses use variants of the breadbox, one of which is described in Chapter Five. The house's need for hot water cannot be met entirely by solar means, so the design employs a backup gas water heater, which is set out of the way in the space behind the loft. This space is also usable for storage, particularly since the down-sloping roof creates an odd shape there. An air shaft above the bathroom, topped by a skylight, rises behind the rear wall of the storage space.

Davis and Benson propose to keep costs down by leaving the interior of the house partially unfinished; the owner would complete interior painting and other finish work. "This firm believes that affordable housing, which incorporates solar heating, can be built and that the two are not mutually exclusive," they have written. "To this end we have designed a plan which is inexpensive and yet very livable."

Chapter Four
The VPS House

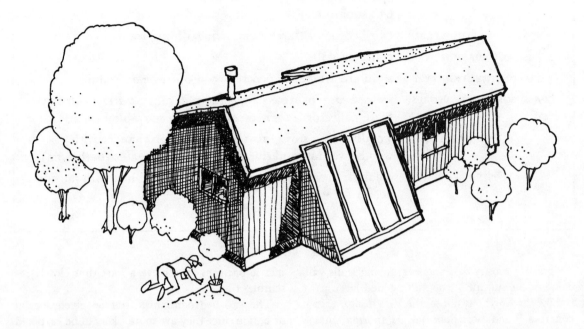

This design is the result of collaboration between a builder and an architect. The concerns and skills of each were tempered and balanced by those of the other. Bob Van Peer is a jack-of-all-trades builder; he's got strong opinions about the waste that puts too much housing beyond affordability, and firsthand knowledge of the costs, qualities, and availability of materials. Bob Schlosser is an architect who has mastered the technical considerations that go with reliance on solar energy, and he wants to implement them in wood, concrete, and glass.

"VPS Associates" didn't exist before the two friends heard about the Cotati contest. After they learned of it, the challenge sparked a winning design; caught without a name for their submission, "VP" and "S" joined initials as they had joined forces. Van Peer and Schlosser live in Mendocino County, the rural northern neighbor of Sonoma County, where Cotati is located. This is significant because they embody a philosophy of rural living, in particular a knowledge of rural housing, that is reflected in their ideas and designs.

"Voluntary simplicity" has instructed thousands of people in many parts of the United States in the realities of living not only without central heating and air conditioning but in some cases without electricity and running water as well. From extremes of self-imposed "deprivation," most of them swing back to a more comfortable way of life —but rarely without having come to appreciate the possibilities of meeting their needs simply. The Mendocino designers brought to their design the conviction that simple living holds fundamental answers to the questions of affordable housing.

"I hope no one ever uses an electric toothbrush in this house," says Bob Van Peer. It's not a fanatic attitude, just a statement which demonstrates his idea that the way people live in it will be a key factor in its ultimate efficiency.

In shape the VPS house is a box lengthened along its east-west axis. Stretching the floor plan this way is much wiser than along the north-south axis. The east and west walls of a house facing due south receive two and a half times more sunshine in summer than in winter; so the heat gain in a

The VPS House

DESIGNER:	VPS Associates
AREA:	642 square feet
FLOOR PLAN:	two bedrooms, large open living/dining room
FOUNDATION TYPE:	concrete slab
CONSTRUCTION TYPE:	standard frame, sloped redwood open-beam ceiling
PASSIVE-SOLAR FEATURES:	*space heat:* concrete slab as thermal mass; *water heat:* flat-plate collector; *other:* recessed entry, movable insulation
BACKUP SYSTEMS:	woodburning stove, air-to-water heat exchanger with woodstove, fan and ducts, electric wall heater (bathroom)
OTHER FEATURES:	colored, incised concrete floor, storage cabinet with outside access

design with mostly east and west-facing walls will come in the summer, when it's needed least.

Like the Northbay house, the VPS design uses a concrete foundation/floor for its thermal mass. Van Peer makes much of the time-saving and cost-cutting virtues of this technique. To build a continuous perimeter concrete foundation requires construction of parallel wooden forms to hold the concrete in place until it has set. Then, after stripping away the forms, a heavy-duty grid of wood members and metal straps is built: the subfloor. Only then can the actual floor be laid.

By comparison, the concrete slab requires forms only along its outside edge. Bolts to anchor wall framing to this floor are placed in the concrete when it's wet; as soon as it has set, the walls can go up. Prior to pouring, a two-inch layer of sand must be put down and thoroughly soaked and a vapor barrier spread across it.

Because the slab is floor as well as foundation, Van Peer and Schlosser lavish extra attention on finishing it attractively. The gritty gray surface, sufficient for many functions that concrete performs, is not very appealing as a living room or bedroom floor. So dyes to develop a reddish-brown earth tone are part of the mix, and finishing techniques that can bring up a glossy surface are used. Afterwards the builders incise the concrete in geo-

metric patterns to achieve a look that closely resembles tile.

The two bedrooms need not be given special attention since they are more likely to be carpeted (by the owner). Carpeting would tend to eliminate the thermal mass value of the concrete in areas reached by sunlight, though, which in this design includes a large area at the center of the floor plan and part of the kitchen on the west.

Here's another fundamental point about the potential of a material for efficient use as a thermal mass. A substance has to have high conductivity as well as high heat capacity. Its conductivity is its ability to distribute heat within itself by conduction — that is, by its molecules bumping each other, transferring heat. Wood and brick have about the same heat capacity. But wood is not a good thermal mass because it doesn't transfer much heat from its surface to its interior. The several kinds of brick have quite different conductivities due to the molecular differences in their ingredients. Bricks with a high magnesium content are superior in this regard.

The bank of four floor-to-ceiling windows on the south is built at a sixty-degree angle and gives the house an uncommon look. These prominent windows continue the south-facing slope of a peaked roof and thus are not overhung by any

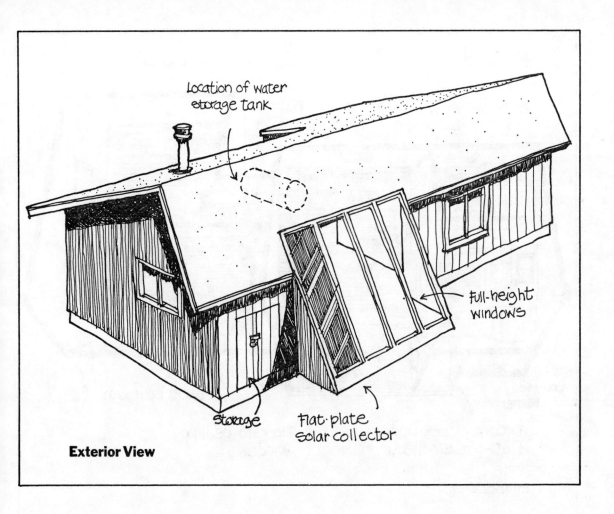

Location of water
storage tank

Full-height
windows

Storage

Flat·plate
solar collector

Exterior View

portion of the house. The roof does shade one conventional window facing south from the master bedroom.

The reason behind the angling of the main windows is simple: the closer a glazed surface is to being perpendicular to the sun's incoming rays, the higher will be the percentage of solar radiation passing through it. At angles away from the perpendicular, greater amounts are reflected off the surface. Actually, the collector surface can be as much as twenty-five degrees from the perpendicular and still admit more than 90 percent of the direct radiation. So a precise angle is not necessarily crucial for excellent performance.

A similar point involves orientation: it's not crucial to face due south, either. The percentage of radiation collected doesn't decrease very sharply up to, again, twenty-five degrees east or west of south. This fact is important and encouraging when it comes to planning a site. Every location has its individual character, and having to face exactly south to get good solar results would be an uncomfortably rigid requirement.

When a designer chooses to angle the solar windows, the rule of thumb is "latitude plus fifteen degrees." In other words, the angle that the plane of the window makes with the ground should equal the latitude of the location plus fifteen degrees. But this again is only meant as a rough guide. Since the sun's height in the sky is always changing along with its apparent motion from east to west — and since the window is fixed — the angle they form is always changing. And it also changes with the time of year, so the chosen angle should strike a reasonable compromise among several contending objectives.

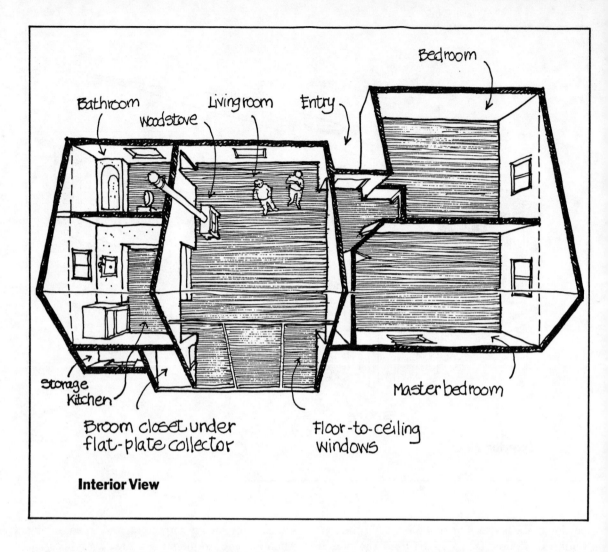

Bedroom

Bathroom   Living room   Entry

Woodstove

Storage
Kitchen

Broom closet under
flat-plate collector

Floor-to-ceiling
windows

Master bedroom

Interior View

Between the contributions of solar energy and, once again, a woodburning stove as a backup source, plenty of heat will build up in the southerly areas of the VPS house. A surplus of heat is likely just from solar input on many days, and a simple layout of ducts, fans, and vents will ship some of it to the bedrooms on the east. (In summer, this system can be used to exhaust air to the outside.)

Even for extended periods of cloudiness, Van Peer and Schlosser are certain the woodstove will heat the entire house. One way to ensure such efficiency stems from a basic decision the designers made about the floor plan. After considering several schemes, they opted for the present, which they consider the simplest of all. In it, circulation areas such as hallways are eliminated or reduced

to a minimum; these cost as much per square foot to build as multipurpose living space. The floor plan is dominated by the large and undifferentiated space on the south, which will certainly be "living room" and "dining room" — but only as the occupants choose to make it, not because of rigid divisions imposed by design. Wood heat reaches most of this open arrangement because there are few obstacles in its path.

The simplification in this design created a situation some people would find inconvenient. A trip to the bathroom requires crossing the open area from either kitchen or bedrooms. But a significant savings is achieved by this choice, too. By placing the kitchen sink and the water-using devices of the bathroom back to back, all the plumbing can be concentrated in the wall that separates them. This is a technique commonly used in manufactured housing, but its good sense can apply in conventionally built houses as well. Snaking pipes under the floor and inside walls to serve sinks, toilets, and showers scattered around the house is not complicated, but it does cost extra, especially in labor. Van Peer and Schlosser think the "long walk" to the bathroom is more than compensated for by these advantages in its location. (Another slight saving results from this plan: when hot water does not have to travel far from heater to faucet, it cools off less than over a longer run — so the water heater is being used more efficiently.)

A small electric heater can be built into the bathroom wall. As far as Bob Schlosser's own needs are concerned, he says, "It's OK for the bathroom to be cold." The point here is that different people find different levels of comfort and convenience adequate, and those differences do not line up as direct evolution from worse to better. While a house built to "too rugged" a level may unnecessarily restrict its potential for many people, it doesn't follow that every house should be built to conventional standards just to ensure its resale value. In fact, the thinking behind the Cotati contest suggests that a large and long-term market for no-frills housing is now emerging.

Hot water for the VPS house is delivered by two separate systems, each a model of ingenious and low-cost simplicity. Flat-plate collectors and heat exchangers are both devices with a broad range of applications in passive-solar designs.

While three of the four large windows on the south are simply glass admitters of solar energy, the fourth is not a window at all but the cover of a flat-plate collector. A flat-plate collector is a shallow box positioned to receive as much sunlight as possible. The cover is transparent; the sides are usually wood with insulation behind. The bottom is made of metal painted black or another dark, heat-absorbing color. (The paint is manufactured specifically to have this characteristic.) Bonded to the metal and coated with the same paint are vertical metal pipes set parallel every few inches.

Solar energy passing through the glass cover is trapped inside the collector — the greenhouse effect in miniature — and absorbed by the dark

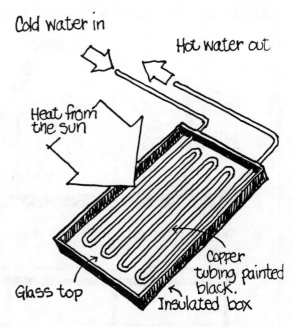

A Flat-Plate Collector

metal sheet and pipes. Water in the pipes is heated by conduction, quite commonly reaching temperatures of 180°F and more. This hot water rises in the pipes by convection, a term which describes the flow of heated water as well as heated air.

The pipes join at the top of the collector and from there a single pipe runs to a storage tank, usually a standard water heater. Similarly, a single pipe connects the tank to the plumbing joint from which the collector pipes diverge. Hot water entering the top of the full tank from the top of the collector displaces cooler water, which returns from the base of the tank to the base of the collector. Thus solar energy alone circulates water through this closed system by a process called thermosiphoning. While the sun shines, water throughout the system gradually heats up. When hot water is drawn off for use in sinks and showers, it is replaced in the tank by cold water from the house's water supply and then heated.

For the system to function properly, the bottom of the storage tank must be at least one foot *above* the top of the collector. This essential factor necessitates making room for the tank in unconventionally high locations. (This is true only for thermosiphoning; the addition of pumps to the

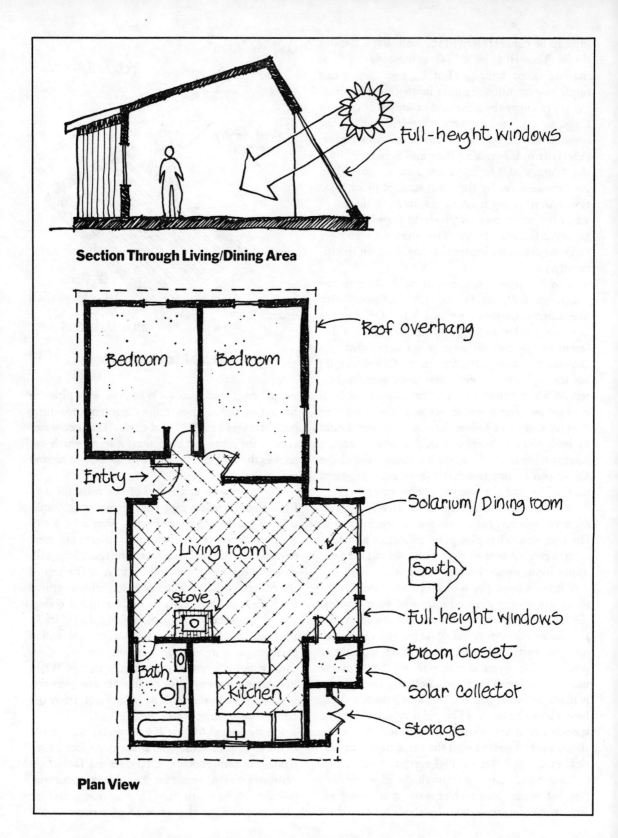

Section Through Living/Dining Area

Full-height windows

Roof overhang

Bedroom

Bedroom

Entry →

Solarium/Dining room

Living room

South

stove

Full-height windows

Bath

Broom closet

Solar collector

Kitchen

Storage

Plan View

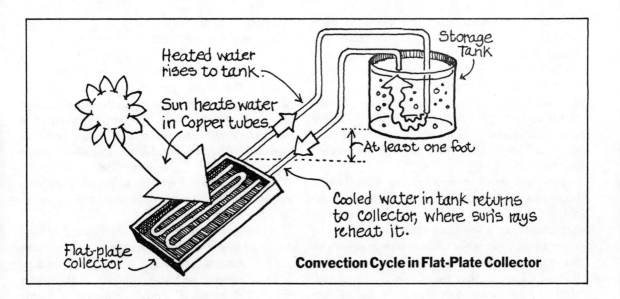

Heated water rises to tank.

Sun heats water in copper tubes.

Storage Tank

At least one foot

Cooled water in tank returns to collector, where sun's rays reheat it.

Flat-plate collector

Convection Cycle in Flat-Plate Collector

system makes it possible to move water in any desired direction.) In the VPS house, the tank is built into a small attic space right behind, and a bit above, the collector. Extra lumber and bracing support the weight of the full tank, which is wrapped in an insulating jacket.

At night, of course, the collector cools off. As hot water is used during the evening, it is replaced by cold water that is not being heated by the collector; this replacement lowers the overall temperature of water in the tank and may deplete the supply of hot water until the collector is again in operation.

In some designs, the tank remains fully operable as a gas or electric hot water heater that can be turned on at night or on cloudy days. Typically this arrangement is automatic: the collector is regarded as a preheater, and whenever the temperature of the water in the tank falls below a certain level, the heater switches on.

The VPS tank can also be heated by the second system, which consists of a small metal box built into the woodstove. Water in this box is heated by air rising from the fire below (when there is one!). Like the plumbing of the flat-plate collector, the box is connected by pipes to inlet and outlet openings on the same storage tank. Thermosiphoning again causes water in the box and pipes to circulate continuously.

The metal box is a kind of heat exchanger.

Heat exchangers, in an endless variety of forms, appear again and again in solar designs as a means of making heat in one form available in another. Some heat is lost in the exchange, but for a job as small as domestic water heating it is quite reliable. (Using homemade or kit heat exchangers of this type, many back-to-the-landers enjoy hot showers even though they don't have electricity or natural gas.)

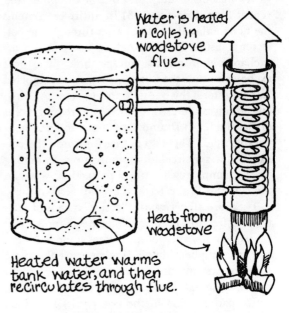

Water is heated in coils in woodstove flue.

Heat from woodstove

Heated water warms tank water, and then recirculates through flue.

Woodstove Heat Exchanger

Since the woodstove will be used at times when solar energy isn't sufficient to heat the house, this source of hot water will at those same times make up for the inactivity of the collector. Nevertheless, some mornings will find the storage tank full of lukewarm water. From the designers' point of view this is another quite acceptable reality. "The occupants may have to heat some water on the cookstove or light another fire," is Bob Van Peer's comment.

Both hot water systems involve hazards that occupants will have to be alert to. The hazards are not to themselves but to the equipment. With the heat exchanger, it's necessary that there always be water in the pipes while a fire is burning—or else the metal may be damaged. Valves in the line are normally open so that water can fill the pipes; after any maintenance or repairs to this plumbing, then, they must be reopened.

The second hazard is not melting but freezing. In fact, keeping the water in flat-plate collectors from freezing is a major consideration for solar designers. Several methods are commonly used. (1) Automatic controllers switch on when they sense imminent freezing conditions and recirculate water, from storage, through the collector pipes. (2) Draindown systems also use sensors to note an oncoming freeze; they respond by opening valves that drain the water out of the pipes and vent it from the system. (3) In antifreeze systems the nonpotable fluid that passes through the collector transfers heat to potable water via a heat-exchange loop inside a storage tank. (The heat exchanger inside the woodburning stove is labeled "air-to-water"; this one is "water-to-water.") Various additives are used to lower the freezing point of the fluid. (4) Drainback systems too use nonpotable fluid. These do not let fluid into the collector unless a circulation pump is on. Switching off the pump provides freeze protection: water in the collector drains back to a small reservoir.

These are all necessarily "active" means of solving the freezing problem. The need for special valves, sensors, and pumps creates a more expensive and complicated unit. Truly passive flat-plate collector systems can operate only in mild climates. (Manual draindown is possible with the active participation of the occupant.) Breadbox systems, however, which hold a greater volume of warmed water at the point of collection, can withstand brief freezing spells (such as occur at Cotati).

With regard to cooling the house, efficiency will require that some type of insulating shades be used to reduce heat loss through the large windows at night and to block sunlight from entering through them on hot days. The central windows can be insulated by movable shades mounted near the ceiling inside. The shades pull down and make a tight seal with the wood framing that supports the glass. (There's more discussion of movable insulation in Chapter Five.)

According to solar researcher Edward Mazria (some of whose data Bob Schlosser used to make his calculations for Cotati), a single thickness of glass with nighttime insulation (such as the shades in the VPS house) is nearly as effective as double glazing at the high latitudes of Seattle, Madison, and New York. Double glazing locks a dead air space between two panes of glass. Although this arrangement definitely decreases heat loss, the double thickness also reduces the transmission of solar radiation—heat gain—by absorbing more. It's a question of tradeoff that will be answered best by considering specific climate and location. For a cold climate such as New England's, double-paned windows are well worth having. Even triple glazing, which is double glazing plus a storm window, may be worth the cost. But in a sunny place such as Albuquerque, Mazria says, single glazing with night insulation actually outperforms double glazing with night insulation: the difference in gain is greater than the difference in loss.

A common-sense way by which design can modify heat loss is to place little-used parts of the house at its margins, particularly on the north. A clothes closet, for example, puts an additional volume of air and many pounds of clothing between the outside and the interior where occupants actually live.

Two features of the VPS design make efficient use of remote spaces. Because the flat-plate collector casts shade onto the interior, the concrete behind it cannot function efficiently as thermal mass. This shading and the fact that its south wall slopes make this an odd space, which the designers have designated as a roomy "broom closet" with access from the living room.

Adjacent to this space, on the southwest corner of the house, is another storage area. In this case access is only from the outside, making it useful mainly for garden and car tools, lawn chairs, garden hose, and the like. Because it is not meant to be reached from inside, during construction it can be sealed around its interior to make it an effective thermal buffer.

The kitchen is laid out compactly along the west wall. Part of the incised concrete floor extends into the kitchen because midmorning sun will strike it directly in winter. A counter with cabinet space beneath defines the kitchen apart from the living/dining area, but food, heat, and conversation can pass easily over the counter top. Heat from the range and refrigerator motor also raise the temperature here.

The small, low-cost house does not preclude having additional space, especially later on as the family grows. A good design for such a house anticipates future growth by specifying where it should take place and making the addition as uncomplicated as possible. The VPS design projects a third bedroom to be built on the northwest. This would be a chilly location. But the designers also envision a greenhouse attached to the south wall of the master bedroom, and this would supply enough heat to the present bedrooms that the surplus from the central area could be passed through ducts to the new bedroom.

In adding the greenhouse, some walls would have to be removed to link the master bedroom to the greenhouse. Presumably the new wall would contain large glass doors so that the sun could

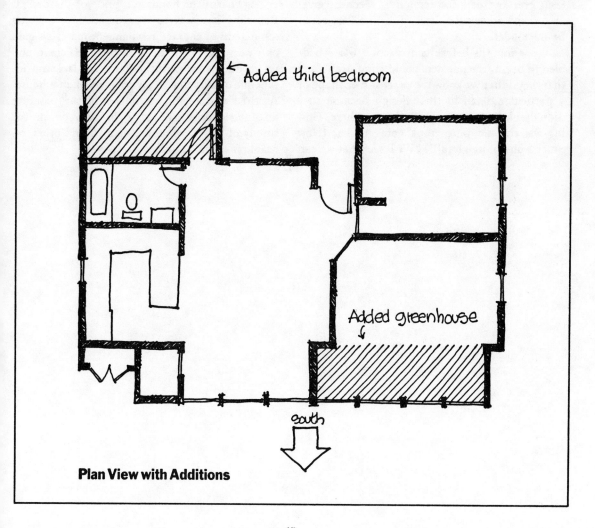

Added third bedroom

Added greenhouse

south

Plan View with Additions

shine directly into large areas of the bedroom. At that point some of the bedroom floor would function as more thermal mass.

The present entry on the north is set back several feet to gain protection from the elements. This setback provides most of the wall surface of the enclosed porch that Van Peer and Schlosser picture being built there in the future. Enclosure would create a double entry, an excellent scheme for reducing the substantial heat loss created by people coming and going. It would be a mud room, too, a place for heavy coats and boots.

Using available materials, particularly recycled ones, is another integral part of the VPS approach to affordable housing. Many people who do a lot of building practice the venerable habits of rummaging and hoarding and, so, have developed keen eyes and ears for remnants, seconds, giveaways, and other good deals. Bob Van Peer could be the model.

A few months before construction was scheduled to begin, the partners could comfortably say that they didn't yet know the exact size or shape of a particular detail in their design because they didn't yet know what they'd find to use there. How big was the hot water tank going to be? (How much would it weigh full?) "We'll see what we can come up with — and if it's too big, I'll cut one end off and weld it smaller," Van Peer promised.

He had his eye on some material that was going to waste — and shouldn't because it apparently could be used as first-rate insulation. Overseas shipments to Bay Area ports sit on styrofoam pallets that are routinely thrown away after the cargo is unloaded. These rigid, two-inch-thick panels have, to recyclers like Van Peer, obvious value, and throwing them away comes close to being a crime. For the cost of fetching them he might show a nice savings and demonstrate a useful idea to whomever takes notice.

Because Van Peer already had some impressive redwood beams that would be difficult to find new let alone afford, Schlosser chose not only to use them but to emphasize them in an open-beam ceiling that is the handsome pride of the design. Recycling is a way to incorporate into a house some items of character which new materials gain only with age. No matter how clean, efficient, and up to date, new construction often lacks an intangible quality that many people seek in a house. As tired and inefficient houses of the past are abandoned or scheduled to be torn down, the supply of doors, windows, boards, and other reusable materials grows.

Chapter Five
The Open Plan House

The roles of house designer, builder, and owner are not new for women; Diana Samhradh, a journeywoman carpenter, Bonnie Pencek, a solar technician, and Georgia Stubbs, a designer-draftswoman, are another winning team in the Cotati contest. In dozens of cultures throughout the world women have traditionally taken primary responsibility for the tasks of dwelling design and construction.

To meet contemporary needs as emphasized in the contest, the three women pooled their skills to create the design for this gambrel roof house. The gambrel roof gives the house a less stark profile than several of the other designs; it enfolds the interior space. The choice of roof is practical in that it allows a large, tall loft space, a crucial feature over a first floor of only about 550 square feet.

The kitchen, relative to the total area, is quite large and open. Unlike most of the other floor plans in the book, this one places the kitchen in the solar direct-gain area, an indication that it's a place likely to be occupied much of the time. It's on the east, where the first cooking and eating of the day can be done in pleasant morning light.

Except for the bathroom, the floor plan of this design is not differentiated into rooms. The kitchen is identifiable, of course, by its work area; but its space is not marked off from the dining area, which in turn flows unhindered into the living room. The purpose of the open floor plan is to aid the flow of air and heat and to create a feeling of spaciousness. A bay window in the west wall is an appealing feature; a long built-in bench in front of it is a window seat with storage space beneath it.

A woodstove stands near the center of the floor, where it can most efficiently radiate heat to the compact house. While a fire burns, the towering stovepipe will be a heat-radiating object rising through the middle of the air space.

Recognizing the privacy problems that an open floor plan can raise, the plan designates an out-of-the-way area as a quiet room. Placement of the walls to support the stairway and the location of the entry leave this corner almost totally shielded from the rest of the house. An area of only about forty square feet, it clearly does not need to be large to accomplish its intended function. In fact,

The Open Plan House

DESIGNERS:	Georgia Stubbs, Bonnie Pencek, Diana Samhradh
AREA:	552 square feet plus 245 square feet (loft)
FLOOR PLAN:	mainly open on first floor with open loft accessible by stairway
FOUNDATION TYPE:	continuous perimeter concrete
CONSTRUCTION TYPE:	standard frame, plywood finished floor
PASSIVE-SOLAR FEATURES:	*space heat:* water drums as thermal mass; *water heat:* breadbox; *other:* air-lock entry, movable insulation
BACKUP SYSTEMS:	woodburning stove, air-to-water heat exchanger with woodstove, gas water heater
OTHER FEATURES:	quiet room; recycled doors, windows

its size may well be a virtue in providing a retreat. Incidentally, a trapdoor here gives access to the crawl space.

The house sits on a continuous perimeter concrete foundation and uses a conventional grid of joists to support the floor and carry R-19 insulation. In addition, three pier-and-post structures near the midline of the foundation provide support for the extra load of the loft. This type of foundation was chosen by the design team because the site originally chosen for construction appeared to have a drainage problem and because they preferred a wood rather than a concrete floor.

A major cost savings is realized by making what is usually regarded as a subfloor the finished floor. Tongue-and-groove plywood 5/8 inch thick is nailed to the joists — and that's it. In conventional construction, this layer would in turn be covered by hardwood, tile, or carpeting; any of these materials can be added later, but the designers regard the plywood as sufficient for a start and think plenty of potential homeowners will too.

There are many kinds of plywood, each meant to perform a different job. Diana Samhradh says that "plugged and touch-sanded AC grade" is a type that's been finished enough at the plywood mill to serve as a livable floor surface. Sanding has

already smoothed it and football-shaped plugs give it an interesting appearance. Staining it is easy finishing work for the owner. Area rugs are a much less expensive way than wall-to-wall carpets to add color, texture, and softness to a floor. The area around the woodstove should be kept free of rugs and carpeting, since ashes and bits of wood inevitably fall to the floor. The stove itself must stand on fireproof material.

Structural integrity in this design calls for a truss to support the roof and to tie in the north and south walls. A truss can be built in place or prefabricated on-site or off-site and lifted into place. Made of large-dimension lumber arranged in triangles and held together by steel plates and bolts rather than nails, a truss is engineered to span distances and support roof loads that ordinary rafter arrangements cannot. The scissors truss in this design is located midway between the loft edge and the west exterior wall.

The decision that ruled out the concrete slab and a concern for economics led to the use of water in barrels as the structure's thermal mass. Eight 55-gallon drums, mounted on casters with brakes, stand just inside the south wall. Painted dark green, the barrels will absorb solar radiation and, transferring heat to the water by conduction, store it for radiation into the room at night. Re-

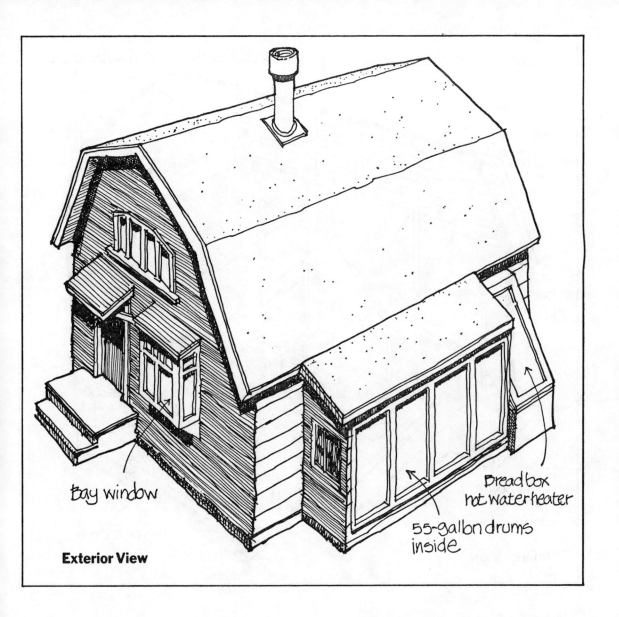

Bay window

Bread box
hot water heater

55-gallon drums
inside

Exterior View

cycled from their original use as containers of oil, these drums are fitting elements in a renewable energy system.

There are many other ways to use water as the heat storage medium. Translucent plastic cylinders let light reach the water directly and are lighter and more attractive than drums as a decorative element. (Georgia Stubbs doesn't just accept the 55-gallon drums for their inexpensive practicality—she thinks they're appropriate and playful. On the living area side the solar water barrels will be painted with a mural.) More primi-

tive experiments involve stacked water-filled glass bottles and even black-painted bleach containers in the path of the sun's rays to serve as thermal mass.

The woodstove radiates additional heat to the thermal mass, which will contribute to warmer temperatures in the very early morning. The efficiency of this sort of secondary heating ability is difficult to measure except in actual practice.

The entry is an unheated "air lock." With its doors closed it is cut off from both the warm interior and the cold exterior of the house. The dead

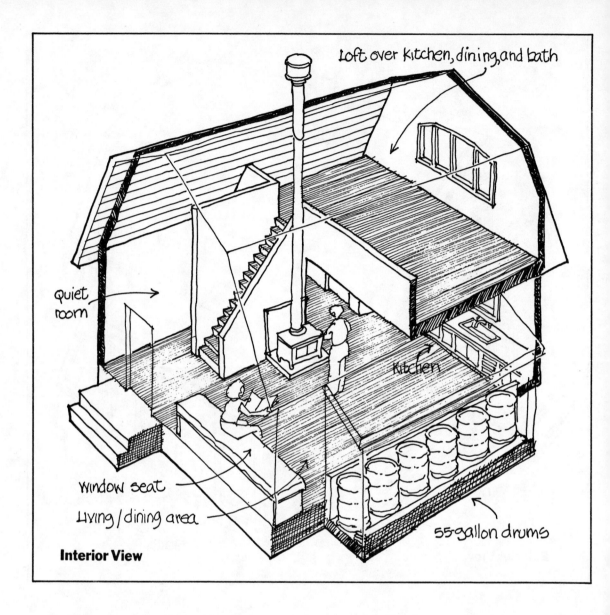

Loft over kitchen, dining, and bath

quiet room

Kitchen

Window seat

Living / dining area

55-gallon drums

Interior View

air inside it acts as a buffer and reduces heat losses caused by entrances and exits from the house.

Placing the bathroom on the north side of the house was another conscious choice intended to aid the heating system. Because the actual amount of time spent in this room is small, it's appropriate to put it relatively far from the heat sources and in a position where it too can act as a buffer.

Water is heated in this design by one of the simplest of solar devices, the breadbox water heater. The breadbox in its basic form is a tank in a box: the plane of the box which faces the sun is glass.

Like the thermal-mass drums, the tank absorbs direct solar radiation, which heats the water inside it. The breadbox tank is plumbed to a backup source (conventional water heater). The tank is painted black, but the inside of the insulated box presents a shiny surface to the sun so that it can reflect energy toward the tank.

In this design the breadbox stands at the southeast corner of the house. Actually, this is a two-tank breadbox system. Cold water enters the first tank and is heated by the sun. The warmed water from the first tank moves into the second tank and

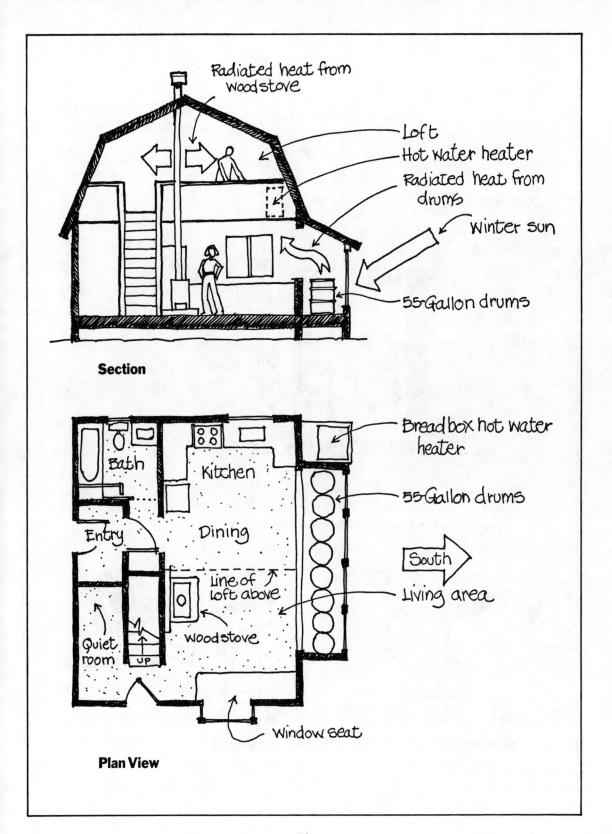

Section

Radiated heat from woodstove

Loft
Hot water heater
Radiated heat from drums
Winter sun
55 Gallon drums

Plan View

Bread box hot water heater
55 Gallon drums
South
Living area

Bath
Kitchen
Dining
Entry
Line of loft above
Woodstove
Quiet room
UP
Window seat

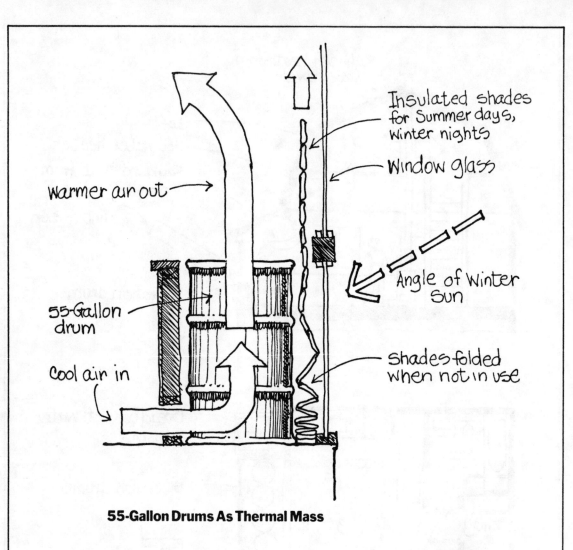

Warmer air out →

Insulated shades for Summer days, winter nights

Window glass

55-Gallon drum

Angle of Winter Sun

Cool air in

Shades folded when not in use

55-Gallon Drums As Thermal Mass

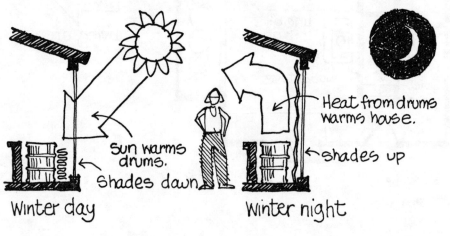

Sun warms drums. Shades down

Heat from drums warms house.

shades up

Winter day

Winter night

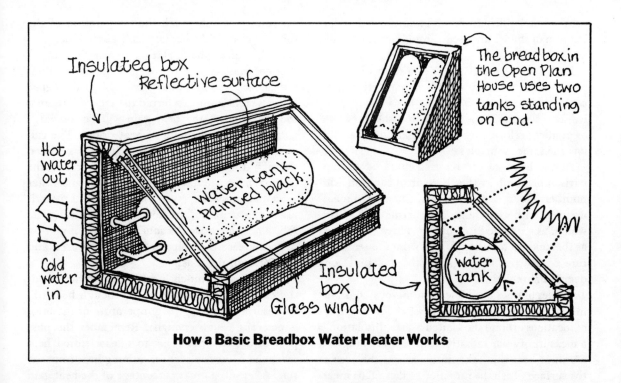

Insulated box
Reflective surface

Hot water out

Cold water in

Water tank painted black

Insulated box
Glass window

The breadbox in the Open Plan House uses two tanks standing on end.

Water tank

How a Basic Breadbox Water Heater Works

is heated even further before going into the conventional or backup water heater located in the loft. No pumps or controls are used in the breadbox system. Heated water is moved by convection and city water pressure. The woodstove is a second source of hot water by means of a heat exchanger similar to the one described in the VPS house.

As in the VPS house, the roof design does not present sufficient overhang to shade the south windows completely in summer. This arrangement appears to violate a cardinal principle of passive-solar design. But design rules, if not made to be broken, can at least be lived up to in more than one way. That the roof must overhang each southern window by a precise distance would be far too rigid a rule and impose too narrow a range of possibilities. The major alternative is to use some kind of movable shade or shutter. Obviously shades and shutters are a very old method of keeping out the sun; but in this instance the old idea has been reexamined and modernized. The key is to achieve a high insulating value and a snug seal around the edges of the glass, the surface where most heat enters and leaves the house. Movable insulated shades or shutters do work that traditional curtains and drapes never did.

Manufacturers sell many varieties of this important new product. One example, which is slightly adapted for use in the barrel area of this design, is the Warm Window developed in Seattle. Essentially it is a multilayer sandwich of flexible materials, each included to perform a specific job of heat retention/reflection. The Warm Window consists of a layer of fiberfill fused to Mylar for heat reflectance; a plastic vapor barrier layer to control heat-filled moisture from escaping; a thin fiber insulation layer; and a lining resistant to mildew and ultraviolet light. Tightly woven decorator fabric is added to face the shade, magnetic strips are included in the edge hems for a magnetic sealing, and the composite is then made into a traditional roman shade folding horizontally.

Thermal shades are mounted in this design to open and close in a reverse direction (that is, they open downward), aided by a pulley system. This will allow shading of the water barrels to prevent excessive summer heat gain while still permitting some natural daylight to enter. When winter gain is required, the shades completely fold open to expose the barrels.

Naturally the shades will also be in use on a typical winter night, when the house's heat sources are the water-filled drums and woodstove. Insulating roman shades are used throughout the house, not just on the south-facing windows.

Each winning design included a study of its own performance which projected a theoretical percentage of heat supplied to the house by its passive-solar system. These studies, and the ones used to predict performance in any solar home, all follow the same principles.

At the heart of the figuring must be a comparison of numbers that measure heat gain with numbers that measure heat loss. The unit of measurement for both is the British thermal unit (Btu), which, as explained in Chapter Three, is defined as the amount of heat that will raise the temperature of one pound of water (about a pint) one degree Fahrenheit.

Tables of data available in numerous books list insolation (not insulation) statistics for hundreds of locations around the United States. Insolation is a measure of solar radiation expressed in langleys, a unit of heat that takes into account the area of the surface which the radiation strikes. This measure can be converted, in turn, to Btus per square foot.

Insolation data reflect the latitude of a location. Other tables list the average monthly temperature at those hundreds of locations (from which each place's number of degree-days can be calculated). By knowing how much solar radiation is available during a particular month, how much the average temperature must be raised to achieve a steady indoor temperature (65°F), and how much glazing the house has facing south, a rough but useful number for heat gain — Btus per day — can be figured.

There are many other factors to consider as well. Glazing does not admit all the radiation, so a standard fraction is removed according to whether the window is single pane, double pane, and so forth. If the house faces a direction very far from south, this too is figured in; so is insolation through east and west windows. Shade cast by trees and additional gain from reflectors can also be accounted for.

By combining the heat gain figure with heat capacity and volume of the house's thermal mass, a separate calculation determines the amount of this radiation that will be stored. This calculation

also indicates how much the temperature of the thermal mass will fluctuate as it absorbs heat.

At the design phase, glazing area and volume of thermal mass can be changed if the calculations indicate operational problems. This is the "glass to mass" relationship referred to earlier. If there is too much glass, the heat gain will be too large compared to the amount of heat stored. The calculations imply that if too much heat is gained through the windows, the temperature of the thermal mass will have to climb farther and faster than it actually can, given the nature of its material. In this situation the house will overheat. The solution is to reduce the square footage of glazing or to increase the volume (the surface area and thickness) of the mass.

If there is too much mass, on the other hand, the calculations imply that not enough heat will be absorbed (that is, the temperature of the mass is not raised high enough). Remember the purpose of the thermal mass: to release stored heat when the house is no longer gaining heat from the sun. After all, a great percentage of the heat gain will become heat loss after sunset as heat starts to travel through surfaces and cracks toward the colder environment outside. The thermal mass must have stored enough of the gained heat to replace heat as it is lost.

Figuring heat loss is as simple in principle but more complex in practice than figuring heat gain. The complexity stems mainly from the fact that each surface has a different propensity to let heat escape. The type of construction and the amount of insulation in a wall as well as its surface area must all be considered. Floors and roofs lose heat at different rates than walls. Uninsulated windows are the real escape hatches, allowing much more heat loss than the walls around them. As with heat gain, the difference between average outdoor and desired indoor temperatures is part of the calculation.

Research has converted all these variables into standard numerical factors, however, and figuring total heat loss essentially means adding up all the separate heat losses for each area and type of surface. With total heat gain and loss numbers in hand, we can determine rough percentages for the contribution and the need for auxiliary heat. Bonnie Pencek, a solar energy technician, prepared the study that accompanied the design. She writes, "The heating and cooling study of our house is based on the performance calculations of three seasonal months of the year: January, March, and August. Calculations are theoretical projections of actual performance, yet they give some idea of how the house can function."

For January, Bonnie Pencek figured a solar energy gain (through south windows on a sunny day) of 102,211 Btus per day. Heat loss is estimated at 91,199 Btus per day. This is a net gain of 11,012 Btus per day. Some 440 gallons of water (eight 55-gallon drums) will store 3,665 Btus with every one-degree rise in water temperature; with 11,012 Btus to store, this means the temperature of the mass will rise about 3°F.

If every day of January were sunny, the house would gain 112 percent of the energy needed to maintain an average indoor temperature of 65°F. Since statistics predict fifteen sunny days in January in Cotati, this analysis says that solar energy will provide 54 percent of the total heat needed for the month. Table 4 shows the calculations for March. For August, the study concludes, "No heating is required in August and it has been determined that the thermal mass is adequate storage to absorb excess ambient heat, provided that the shades are used during the day."

TABLE 4
PASSIVE-SOLAR PERFORMANCE FOR MARCH

Solar heat gain = 86,486 Btu/day
Heat loss = 58,750 Btu/day
Net gain = 27,736 Btu/day
Thermal mass storage = 3,665 Btu/°F
(same as January)
Thermal mass
temperature fluctuation = 27,736 ÷ 3,665 = 7.57°F
$$\frac{86,486}{58,750} \times \frac{15 \text{ sunny days}}{31 \text{ days}} = 71\%$$ solar energy contribution to maintaining average 65°F indoor temperature in March

---

In analyzing the cooling operation, it's assumed that there's *no* direct gain of solar energy because overhangs and shades are blocking it out. Ventilation becomes the key; it's measured in terms of volumes and velocity of air flowing through the house.

Summer overheating is surely a circumstance that has to be planned for. All east and west windows in the house will be openable to allow ventilation. In addition, the thermal shades in the sun space will prevent direct heat gain to the water barrels. There's also a skylight on the northern ceiling in the loft. A virtue of having the main entry on the north is that the main source of air for ventilation will come in from that shaded side of the house.

Instead of adding a room outside the existing floor plan to expand this house, the designers would complete the second floor and instead of a loft have two separate bedrooms with either movable partitions or openable interior windows to facilitate ventilation. In this case, the stairwell would channel cool north air to the second story.

A two-story house is, of course, an economical means of occupying expensive land; to achieve full use of the second story a broad peaked roof of some kind is needed, such as the gambrel of this design.

Georgia Stubbs believes a fan might be needed to assist natural convection for heating as well as cooling. As the owner of such a house she says she would definitely build trellises on the southwestern and western perimeters of the house. By training perennial, deciduous vines up a network of thin wooden poles, she'd create a sunscreen that would be of real shade value as well as attractive landscaping. Grapes and wisteria are plants that will do well in many locations. Since it takes these plants several years to get well established, a bamboo shade could be used on the outside of the wall during that time if overheating was a problem.

Annual vegetable gardening can be relied upon to produce temporary shading from midsummer to fall. Close-in planting of pole beans, for example, growing up tall and dense, casts a solid shadow. Carefully staked tomatoes, close ranks of corn, and morning glories and other flowers will all do nearly as well. This approach to landscaping ties the house to the ground with an organic connection. The site plan (see the appendix) leaves common areas to be developed by all the occupants working as an association. A community garden makes great sense in such a space, either tended jointly or divided into individual plots.

An idea put forward by this team of women is to use the "gray water" — water from sinks, tubs, and showers — on gardens or other plantings in the little community or around the house. Although this practice is not allowed under local health codes, it was done commonly during the California drought of 1977 and may be necessary as a means of dealing with the next drought when it occurs. This ban is another point of rigidity in the code system, which the designers were urged to challenge by the original announcement of the contest.

Returning to the house, two details of the structure also challenge codes. The first concerns fire prevention. Safety considerations have led to building code regulations dictating the minimum distance a woodstove can be from the nearest protected wall, as well as the type of material one may use to protect a wall. Few would deny that this is a legitimate and humane concern, yet it can restrict appropriate designs that meet equivalent safety standards. Citing a design in the book *Wood Heat Safety*, the designers propose using a four-inch brick wall with a one-inch air space between the brick and the finished wall surface. Metal ties would be used to secure the brick to the stairway framing, which would be covered with gypsum wallboard. The woodstove would thus be located at the code minimum of twelve inches from the wallboard surface. Given discretion to judge this installation, some building inspectors will permit this type of wall protection; but others will toe the literal line of the code and disallow it. This is a gray area, but it does illustrate a type of problem that arises fairly often now — and will arise much more often as buildings use more innovative, energy-efficient design.

Somewhat less obvious than the need for fire prevention is the need for regulations which control the height of beams and lofts. According to Diana Samhradh, the local code calls for seven feet six inches while the designers specify seven feet to the underside of the loft beam and seven feet three inches to the underside of the second-floor joists. Should the whole building be redesigned to bring this "flaw" up to code?

Here again a specific example highlights a major issue of the near future. As more people take the matter of shelter back into their own hands the inadequacies of certain code regulations will become more obvious — and the need to revise them more urgent.

Chapter Six
The Double Envelope House

Randy Greenwald compares his design to the Volkswagen Beetle. When that famous "people's car" was first introduced, people found it odd, disconcertingly small, almost ugly. But from that low point, its popularity grew stupendously; it became perhaps the most influential automobile design of its time and its "ugliness" became beauty in the minds of millions. In anticipating the small, efficient, unglamorous cars that fill American roads today, the VW was an avant-garde design that created new standards in cars rather than trying to measure up to old ones.

The small passive-solar house of the eighties, Randy Greenwald predicts, is an embryonic Beetle. It anticipates the trend of future housing far more accurately than the glamorous, all-convenience house at the "top of the line" today. And, in due time, its values will suggest a new aesthetic according to which it will be perceived as, in its own way, beautiful.

It's a fact that many designs for solar homes disturb some people: odd concentrations of glass, unconventional angles, exotic devices attached to roofs — these are often pronounced ugly and often clash when placed on a street of standard homes. Even the most enthusiastic solar advocate acknowledges this problem, and the new industry's magazines resound with calls and plans for solving it. Most likely the future will see a convergence: a shift of public tastes meeting refinements of solar design. For the present, the Cotati designs are a new breed whose very existence brings that future closer.

Greenwald, who was trained as an architect, chose to work with a heating/cooling system called the "double envelope." This approach not only presents the increasingly familiar bank of glass (vertical not sloped) to the south but also calls for some unconventional building techniques in the rest of the house.

From the peak of the roof to its north edge, and along the entire north wall, the building has two "skins" instead of one. An eight-inch blanket of air space separates an outer skin of insulation and roofing (and siding) from an inner layer of insulation and ceiling (and wallboard). A continuous

The Double Envelope House

DESIGNER:	Randolph Greenwald
AREA:	508 square feet plus 171 square feet (greenhouse)
FLOOR PLAN:	one bedroom, integral greenhouse
FOUNDATION TYPE:	continuous perimeter concrete
CONSTRUCTION TYPE:	standard frame, double envelope enclosing plenum, exceptional insulation
PASSIVE-SOLAR FEATURES:	*space heat:* greenhouse, convection loop, brick floor as thermal mass; *water heat:* flat-plate collector, breadbox; *other:* earth as thermal mass, louver overhangs
BACKUP SYSTEMS:	freestanding fireplace, fan and ducts, gas water heater
OTHER FEATURES:	hot tub, soil floor in greenhouse

perimeter foundation of concrete lifts the floor of the house thirty inches above the ground and seals the crawl space from the environment outside the perimeter.

These three spaces — between ceiling and roof, inside north wall, and crawl space — comprise most of the plenum, the loop of air that wraps the living area of this house. (The east and west walls, with better-than-average R-19 insulation, are of single-skin construction.) The rest of the loop — and the main source of the heat that circulates through it — is a greenhouse solar collector.

A greenhouse can be adapted endlessly to contribute to solar heating (and cooling). It is probably the most common device with which older homes (with good southern exposure) can be retrofitted to take advantage of solar energy. Logically, the greenhouse effect is desired here; through vents or larger openings in its north wall, air heated in the greenhouse can be drawn into the house itself by natural convection or with fans. Closing the vents in the evening allows the greenhouse to cool off more than the rest of the house during the night, an effect which should be expected since so much of its surface area is glass.

In Greenwald's design, a greenhouse occupies the entire southern fourth of the floor plan — an integral part of the house, not an add-on. By retaining the earth floor, Greenwald fully intends the greenhouse to be used for growing. "It's not just for hanging a few pots or for sitting. There is plenty of topsoil available for gardening year round."

In the double envelope design, rather than supplying warmed air directly into the house, the greenhouse's function is to feed it into the plenum. The greenhouse is separated from the living spaces behind it by a wall — part solid, part fixed glass, part glass door. These surfaces rise to the height of the interior ceiling. Above them the air passes between exposed studs into the ceiling-roof section of the plenum.

According to the theory behind the double envelope, this flow of air is all it takes to keep air moving through the complete convection loop.

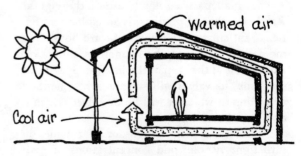

Convection Loop

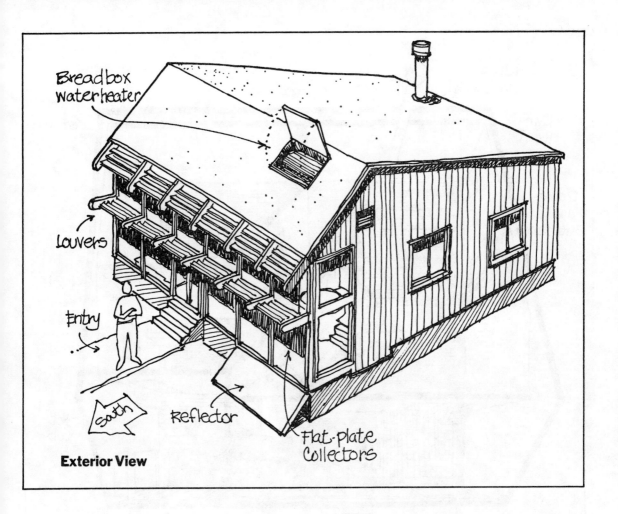

Breadbox
waterheater

Louvers

Entry

South

Reflector

Flat-plate
Collectors

Exterior View

Greenwald reports that the theory is controversial: a Massachusetts professor used computer simulation to demonstrate that it can't work, while actual installations prove that it does!

Clearly, the greenhouse and interior vertical glass allow some direct gain during the day, too. So the design also utilizes some thermal mass. Because the double envelope depends upon an air space beneath the floor, a concrete slab resting directly on the ground is not suitable. This thermal mass is therefore of brick laid over a conventional grid of wooden joists, which in turn are held up by wooden posts anchored in concrete pads or piers. The brick extends from a foot inside the south facade to about the midline of the house; that is, as deep as the sun will strike directly in winter. The northern half of the floor is wood, less expensive than brick and likely to be carpeted

since it isn't thermal mass. Insulation supported by the joists underlies both brick and wood.

The greenhouse is actually split-level. On the west, a pad of brick stands at the same height as the house floor. But stairs lead down from it to the earth itself, which is the "floor" of most of the greenhouse unit. As sod and adobe construction demonstrated on the Great Plains and in the Southwest long ago, earth is a material with valuable heat capacity. It's not as dense as concrete, brick, or stone, but, as Randy Greenwald says, "It's cheap, there's lots of it, and it's right there." (Adobe and rammed earth are compressed bricks of earth, so they're much denser than soil.)

Because the perimeter foundation is uninterrupted and insulated on its exterior surface with a moisture-proof and rodent-proof material, this construction allows the earth *under* the house to

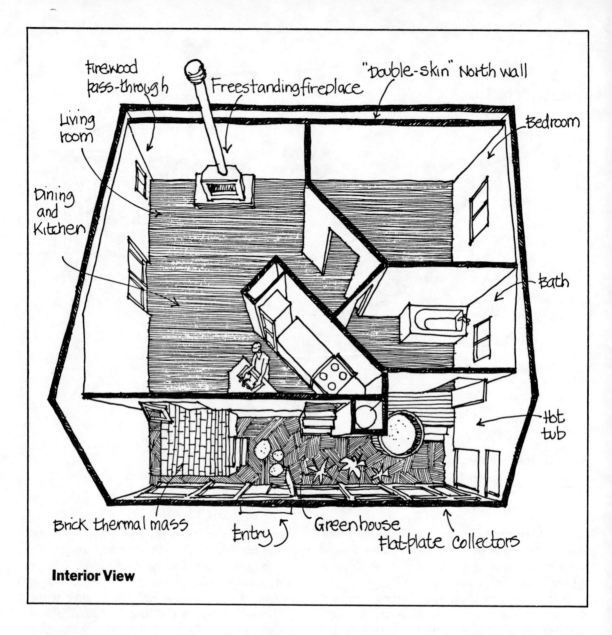

Firewood
pass-through

Freestanding fireplace

"Double-skin" North wall

Living room

Bedroom

Dining and Kitchen

Bath

Hot tub

Brick thermal mass

Entry

Greenhouse

Flat-plate collectors

Interior View

perform fairly efficiently as thermal mass. Heat traveling through the convection loop will be stored in this earth as heated air passes under the floor. Reentering the greenhouse, this air is cooler than it was when it left. But then it is reheated by the sunlight collected there, rises, and passes through the loop again.

Since the foundation is poured into a trench, the soil beneath the house is well protected from the temperature fluctuations outside. Remember: the core of the earth is molten, and heat is radiat-

ing from it toward the surface. In temperate climates, the earth is a steady 55°F ten feet below the surface. This is much warmer than the temperature of night air, so it's a strong basis for useful heat storage. After construction is complete, and as the convection loop operates month after month, the soil temperature in the first few inches below the surface will climb and, Greenwald estimates, never drop below the low sixties. On sunny days it will store thousands of additional Btus for release during the night — a thermal mass.

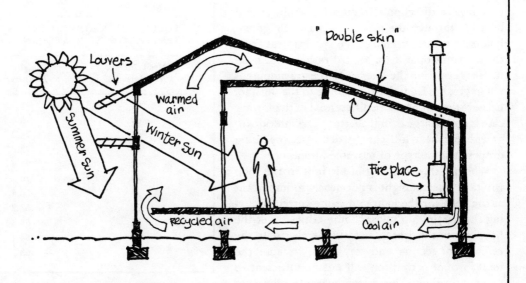

Section

Louvers

"Double skin"

Summer Sun

Winter Sun

warmed air

Fire place

Recycled air

Cool air

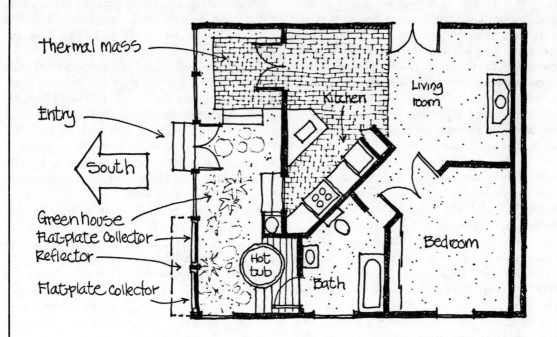

thermal mass

Entry

South

Greenhouse

Flatplate Collector

Reflector

Flatplate collector

Kitchen

Living room

Bedroom

Hot tub

Bath

Plan View

It's possible that at night the convection loop may reverse direction. No entering sunlight and heat loss through the glass may make the greenhouse the coldest stretch of the system; heat from the plenum would drive toward rather than from it. Heat loss from the interior to the greenhouse is not as great as from the greenhouse to the outside, because the temperature differential in the former case is not as large as in the latter. The interior-to-greenhouse heat loss can be decreased by using drapes or some type of movable insulation.

Whether this reversing of air flow in the loop will take place at night is not nearly so important as the need for the loop to operate correctly during the heating-up phase. Some critics think the hot air from the greenhouse will merely rise to the ceiling-roof section and stay there because the total force of convection will not be sufficient to move it further. This certainly would eliminate most of the benefits that the theory promises. To assist the air flow, an eight inch by two foot small-diameter duct and ¼-horsepower fan arrangement can be built into the envelope to pull air down the north wall and under the floor. This mechanical pull will act directly on only a small percentage of the air in the envelope but it will get the entire mass moving in the desired flow, Greenwald believes.

Mean radiant temperature is an expression of the warmth of surrounding surfaces. If the walls and floor of a room are colder than a human body inside it, then the body radiates (loses) heat to them. If the walls and floor are warmer, the reverse is true. Inside a house a higher radiant temperature allows a lower air temperature to produce an equal sensation of comfort.

At night, because the double envelope system warms the walls and crawl space, heat radiates from them toward the objects in the room, notably the people. (So does the brick floor/thermal mass.) In many mechanical heating systems, by contrast, air is first superheated in a furnace and then forced into circulation through living spaces. Occupants feel comfortable because all the air around them is warm. The walls are cold and the heat seeps out through them.

Another difference between these radiant and forced-air approaches to space heating is that, with radiant heat, the air in the room can remain

TABLE 5

EQUIVALENT MEAN RADIANT AND AIR
TEMPERATURES FOR A FEELING OF 70°F

Mean Radiant Temperature	Air Temperature
65	77
66	75.6
67	74.2
68	72.8
69	71.4
70	70
71	68.6
72	67.2
73	65.8
74	64.4
75	63

cooler without any loss of comfort — because the air is not as important a vehicle for heat. If, for example, the mean radiant temperature is 75°F, the air can be 63°F and occupants will *feel* as warm as if all the air were 70°F. Table 5 shows the calculations.

The "wind chill factor" often reported with the weather during the winter is also relevant here. Both temperature differential and wind (natural convection) cause heat loss from body surfaces. A combination of cold and wind makes a body feel colder than the cold would alone. For example, a temperature of 20°F combined with a 20-mph wind causes a loss of body heat equal to the sensation of -10°F with no wind.

Since radiant heating inside a house is less drafty than central heating, it reduces convective heat loss. Greenwald believes that central, forced-air systems actually burn and overdry air, thus producing an environment of less quality than one of fresh moist air. He claims that radiant heat is not only equally comfortable but in fact healthier.

A quite subjective element in house design is the fact that different people report being comfortable at quite different temperatures. These responses are both physiological and "cultural," the result of personal history and the influential opinions of other people. It is also true that people can change somewhat in this regard, as massive public campaigns to lower thermostats attest. Not having to supply heat to warm all the air to the desired comfort level also means that less heat is available to be lost. In short, energy is saved.

During the day, of course, the doors in the wall that separates the greenhouse from the interior can be opened to let in large volumes of warm air. But at the same time, or even with those doors shut, the air in the double envelope is wrapping a blanket of warmth around the interior. Joining two thicknesses of insulation, this blanket creates an extraordinary buffer against fluctuations of the outside temperature. The significant amount of heat generated by lights, cooking, and human bodies will be retained by this superinsulation, too.

The designer does not suggest, even with perfect operation according to the theory, that passive-solar heat will be sufficient in every cold-weather situation. His choice for a backup heating system is a freestanding fireplace installed in the living room against the north wall. Because a traditional fireplace is open, it draws more oxygen than it requires and the wood burns more rapidly than it would in a closed stove. The openness also provides a strong draft that pulls heat from the room and carries it up and away too rapidly through the chimney. In a woodburning stove, metal plates on all sides of the fire are heated and then radiate heat in all directions. The traditional fireplace, by being open to the room, limits its efficiency severely.

Modern versions of the fireplace, however, adopt certain principles of the woodstove. Rather than being built into a wall at the base of a chimney, these fireplaces are freestanding devices which vent smoke through a vertical pipe. (Because the pipe is in the room up to the point where it passes through the ceiling, it too radiates heat.) Solid hinged doors can seal in the fire on the traditionally open side if desired; glass doors can seal the fire and allow the view, too.

In sum, it's a tradeoff, but not so much is lost as with the fireplace of the past. Greenwald says of his choice, "It's a little corny, but I like it. The fireplace has aesthetic value that the most efficient woodstove never will."

Like the Northbay Architects, Greenwald submitted a nearly square floor plan. He says he felt challenged by the task of creating variety and a sense of openness within such a compact design. By using short diagonals near the center of the plan, he laid out the major rooms with uncommon shapes. These present a satisfying complexity without being cluttered or unmanageable.

In this and the other Cotati designs, all the light from the south and the broad view of outdoors tend to create a feeling of greater spaciousness than the actual square footage suggests. This is an optical effect long recognized by designers and often used to practical advantage. By aligning the kitchen counter and appliances diagonally to the main axis of the house, Greenwald deliberately preserved this feature. So someone sitting far up along the northwest wall still has an unimpaired view out through the greenhouse and a pleasant sense of having enough room.

This is a one-bedroom design, conceived less with children in mind than several of the other winners. The "adultness" of it is shown not only by the emphasis on the greenhouse as a true workplace but by the inclusion of a hot tub! "My idea of a great house," the designer says forthrightly, "has a hot tub. Admittedly, here it won't be the finest redwood tub, but . . . There's nothing minimal about this house other than square footage and expense. And I know I could live quite happily in that much space." An incidental benefit from the hot tub is its heat storage capacity, contributing to the overall efficiency of the convective loop.

Solar energy provides hot water to this house by means of two collectors, one passive, one active. A breadbox heater occupies a chunk of south-facing roof and preheats the domestic water supply, which is stored in a water heater in the kitchen. Two flat-plate collectors preheat the hot tub. Both devices utilize reflectors — hinged panels that open away from the collector surface and present reflective faces to the sun. The sun's rays bounce off the shiny surface into the collectors.

Reflectors are an idea that's spreading fast in solar designs, the designer notes. In some plans, they're not only a way to increase collection; moved to a different position they can cover the collector as insulation at night or during cloudy periods. Greenwald will coat his reflectors with an aluminized Mylar sheet or possibly with a paint containing tiny beads, similar to the reflective material used on highway signs.

If access to the reflectors is simple, they can be manually adjusted to whatever angle yields optimal collection of sunlight, which depends on the time of year. If the reflector is fixed, or installed in a remote location (on a roof near a high window, for instance) where it can't be easily reached, less work to be done by the occupant is the tradeoff for less thermal efficiency.

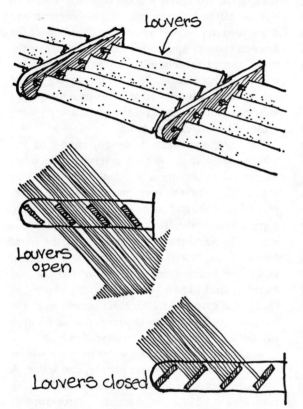

Louvers

Louvers open

Louvers closed

Rather than using a massive second-story overhang to cool this house, Greenwald's design calls on slender wood frames to cast shade on its collector windows. These projections hold one by ten inch louvers, wood slats which can be adjusted via tie-down cords below to open and closed positions, to suit the angle of the sun and the requirements of the situation. It's a very low-tech solution.

The exceptional insulating value of the double envelope will be the main contributor to cooling. Since the design calls for no windows on north or west, the cooling strategy is more to block heat inputs than to vent them. Morning light can enter through openable windows in the east wall.

There are vents high on the east and west walls of the greenhouse. Hot air can escape here. These vents and cool air from beneath the house will keep the loop from overheating.

Two other functional problems—bringing in firewood and getting to the crawl space—are overcome by remarkably simple solutions. Getting firewood into the house is not really a problem, but it's done very directly here through a removable panel on the west wall. With the panel out, firewood can be passed through the wall directly to a storage space beside the fireplace. The sealed perimeter foundation prevents access to the crawl space from outside. The way to get there is from inside: a pair of steps leading from floor level to earth level in the greenhouse is lightweight and removable. (In an alternative scheme, Greenwald proposes to have a removable panel in the foundation on the north. This could be left open in order to allow cool air to enter the convection loop under the house. It would also make storage under the house possible.)

The number of devices people must operate in order for a passive-solar design to work makes an

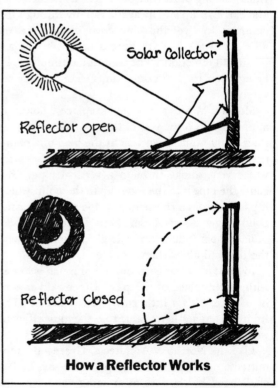

Solar Collector

Reflector open

Reflector closed

How a Reflector Works

important statement about how people will live in such a house. Recalling the prehistory of humans as hunters and gatherers of food, Greenwald looks forward to our being "gatherers of solar energy." Implicit in this remark is a sense that people will live with that energy profoundly in mind, and that they will do naturally what needs to be done to gather and store it.

At the same time, Greenwald recognizes that we live in an age of conveniences and, moreover, that there's no logic in denying them out of overreaction to our energy problems. He doesn't believe mass housing markets are ready for extensive user participation — adjusting reflectors and protecting collectors from freezing — and he wouldn't have called for these techniques in situations less experimental than the Cotati contest. Furthermore, he places considerable trust in the ability of designers to solve passive-solar problems with increasingly convenient solutions.

What people want and what they will adapt to are bits of true information expressed as demands in the marketplace. Housing markets, above all riding on economic forces, are now registering information about what kinds of houses are sensible and right for these and the times ahead.

Chapter Seven
The Solarium House

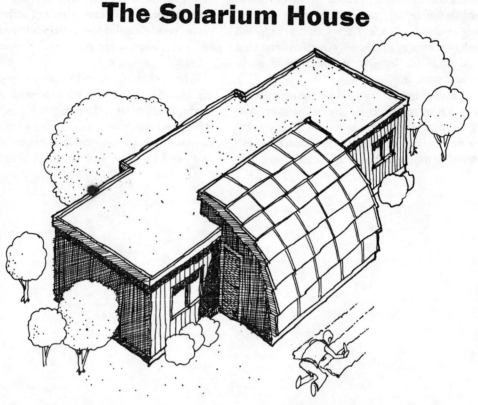

With the solarium design, this book examines a different level of solution to the problems of affordable housing. While employing passive-solar techniques to heat and cool a small and simple house, this design relies upon industrial capability to produce its several prefabricated elements. The extensive research and development lavished on their project by solar consultant/technician Don Moser and designer John Roberts represent an investment that cannot be returned by building a single unit. Instead they saw the Cotati contest as an ideal opportunity to build and demonstrate a house they fully intend to see built, in several models, many times over.

A general survey of the techniques of manufactured housing and the choices available among mobile homes, modular, precut, and kit houses will be found in Chapter Ten. It's important to note here that these techniques and choices are by no means a wholly separate world from the houses at Cotati. Large-scale, factory-based applications

have an essential role to play if affordable housing is to be made available at any rate great enough to meet a tremendous need.

The deeply ingrained prejudice that the end product of industrial housing is either shoddy, monotonous, or ugly must be undone in the minds of millions of Americans. Though not without its elements of truth in some past cases, such prejudice has served to withhold from large segments of the construction industry and the house-buying public the expertise and capacity that the American industrial system has in depth.

The previous four designs can all be categorized as "stick-built." This means that their construction is a wooden framing system comprised of scores of individual wood members—joists, studs, plates, headers, beams, rafters, and more. These members are assembled by hand, a piece at a time, many pieces having been individually processed (shortened, notched, trimmed, and the like) before being assembled. This is a time-consuming process, and when that time is being translated into current union wages, it is a major contributor to the cost of an expensive house.

This type of wooden framing prevails throughout American housing. One deeply appreciated aspect of it is the fact that it can be used by individuals, even untrained individuals working alone. This makes it a valuable tool for exercising personal freedom, of which building one's own home is a truly great expression, as so many do-it-yourself books testify.

But most Americans do not build their own homes and do not want to. The fact that quality housing is built for them by this tedious method is a weakness, not a strength, of the construction industry. In its extreme division of material and labor, stick-built housing can be wasteful, slow, and more costly than it has to be.

Prefabrication is employed in this house design in two quite separate forms: first in the solarium itself, second in the walls of the house. The solarium functions as a greenhouse solar collector, but unlike most greenhouses, which have vertical or angled south walls, this structure curves out from its highest point to reach the ground. Its panes of glass are rigid sheets, but they lie in notches in curving wooden beams. The beams themselves are laminations of many thin strips of western red cedar or Douglas fir made to curve and stick together by an industrial process impossible to duplicate at a building site. Don Moser says he spent three months just on the design and building of the jig, the master mold from which the "glu-lam" beams emerge perfectly dimensioned to receive the glass. Since they take the place of standard structural lumber (whose various capacities can be looked up in standard references), the beams had to be specially engineered and tested for their ability to carry weight and withstand potential wind stress and snow load, as well as for other performance features.

Although various manufacturers supply laminated beams, it took patient research to discover one who could satisfy the special demands of these beams. The beams are designed to be spaced four feet apart for as great a distance as desired. In the Cotati design, the solarium is twenty feet long. The curving face rises to a height of nine feet and covers a depth of twelve feet.

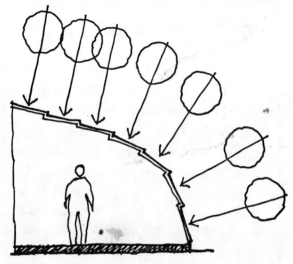

Roberts/Moser Solarium

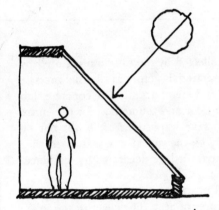

Conventional Solarium

According to Don Moser, the solarium will be a considerably more efficient heat collector than an attached greenhouse with vertical or sloped south walls. The greatest amount of solar radiation passes through glass when the rays are perpendicular to the glass. A standard flat-plate collector or single pane facing south collects the maximum amount of solar energy only a few days each year. But the solarium presents faces at several different angles to the sun and thus achieves a higher efficiency more often. Over large intervals of time, the rays are passing through one perpendicular glass face after another.

The Solarium House

DESIGNERS:	John Roberts, Don Moser
AREA:	680 square feet
FLOOR PLAN:	two bedrooms, integral solar greenhouse
FOUNDATION TYPE:	concrete slab
CONSTRUCTION TYPE:	post-and-beam, prefabricated wall panels
PASSIVE-SOLAR FEATURES:	*space heat:* solarium, water drums, and concrete slab as thermal mass; *water heat:* flat-plate collector; *other:* movable insulation
BACKUP SYSTEMS:	woodburning stove, gas water heater
OTHER FEATURES:	electronic control of hot water systems, curved "glu-lam" beams in solarium, plastic pipe embedded in slab for space heating/cooling control and to supply air to woodburning stove

The heat collected by the solarium is stored by two different materials acting as thermal mass: a concrete slab and metal drums. The concrete slab serves as both floor and foundation for the entire house. The northerly portions of it will not be struck directly by the sun at any season, so they can be carpeted, tiled, or decorated by the placement of area rugs.

Water held in standard 55-gallon metal drums is the other storer of heat. The curve of the solarium creates an interior space near its base that is too low for an adult to stand in without bumping head against glass. Here the design calls for five drums, on their sides, to rest on the concrete. By designing the solarium in this way—the drums keep people at a distance from the lower windows—Roberts and Moser get around the requirement of using 100 percent safety glass ($53 per sheet) and accomplish what they want with 80 percent single-pane glass ($21 per sheet).

In principle, the water thermal mass works just as it does in the open plan design described in Chapter Five; a simple counter is built over the barrels, a place where either plants—or, in this case, people—can bask. This design allows air to circulate around the heated drums. An ingenious,

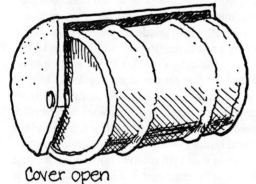

55-Gallon drum with movable insulating cover

Cover open

Cover closed

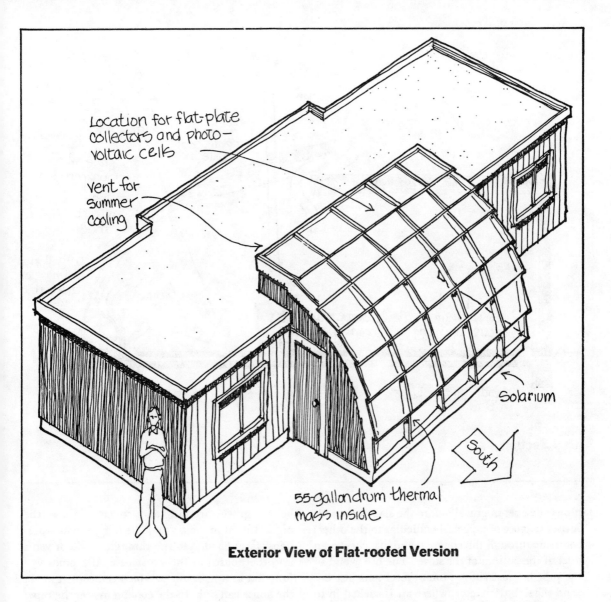

Location for flat-plate collectors and photo-voltaic cells

Vent for summer cooling

Solarium

South

55-gallon drum thermal mass inside

Exterior View of Flat-roofed Version

specially designed insulating cover blocks the drums' nighttime radiation toward the glass and outside. It's a curved shade made of wood and polyurethane insulation and attached to the counter supports with a pivoting hinge. The curve of the shade echoes the curve of the drums: swung back (toward the interior) in the day, it exposes the drums to the sun; at night, in the opposite position, it is a barrier between heat and cold.

A woodburning stove stands in a central position, where it can back up solar heat with wood heat. Don Moser makes an interesting point about woodstoves: the fire's need for oxygen pulls air throughout the house toward the stove. This draw creates a definite pull of cold outside air into the house, too. It may be invisible and a matter of very slight velocities and differences in pressure, but this force strengthens the infiltration of cold air through whatever cracks it can find. Roberts reports that "it adds approximately 20 percent to the heating requirements of a new home built to code."

Even the finest "airtight" stoves have to draw oxygen from someplace. The stove in the solarium house takes its supply directly from outside the house! Here's how: a four-inch-diameter plastic

69

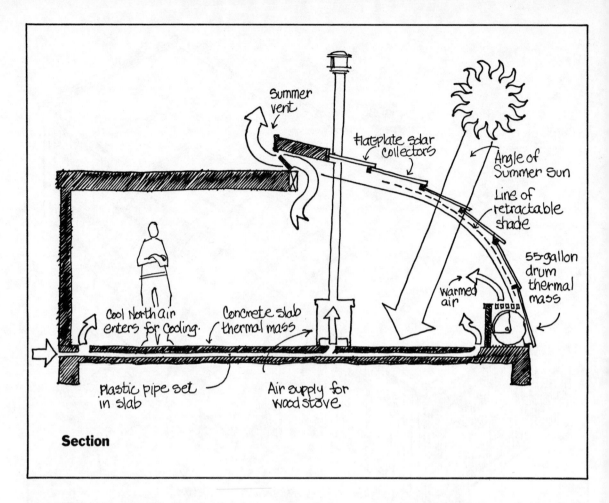

Summer vent

Flatplate solar collectors

Angle of Summer Sun

Line of retractable shade

55-gallon drum thermal mass

Warmed air

Cool North air enters for cooling.

Concrete slab thermal mass

Plastic pipe set in slab

Air supply for wood stove

Section

pipe will be set in gravel before the slab is poured. A riser (a piece of pipe perpendicular to the other) comes up through the concrete and attaches to an inlet at the bottom of the stove. The other end of the pipe lies just above ground level and just beyond the slab perimeter, where air is sucked in to keep the wood burning.

In fact, the entire slab is underlain by plastic pipes in a system that contributes to both cooling and heating. Moser and Roberts admit that this element is something of an experiment, but they regard the relatively minor expense of the plastic pipe as well worth it to see what is gained in efficiency. Running north and south a foot apart, the thirty-two pipes open to the outside on north and south and, through risers, connect to vents in the floor. In a typical winter situation, each pipe (except the one connected to the stove) is capped on the outside. Given the heat capacity of earth

below, gravel around, and concrete above the pipes, the air in them should be fairly warm — perhaps warm enough to rise through the floor vents into the house. In the worst case, the pipes will function as a reservoir to which the coolest air in the house can sink. In the cooling mode, the pipes are uncapped and ground-level air is then drawn through them into the house. Because there are so many pipes, plenty of fine tuning is possible (for heating and cooling) by opening and closing the pipes in various combinations. A screen over the end of each pipe prevents rodent or other invasion. Although the pipes are an experiment, their addition will be easily accomplished by placing them in the base rock prior to pouring the slab floor.

John Roberts points to a common occurrence that has limited the implementation of solar devices and designs. He says that these are usually extras when they're called for at all, and when a designer or architect shows the total price tag to a client, the "solar stuff" is often the first thing cut in the urgent effort to trim the construction budget.

In Roberts and Moser's Cotati design, however, the solarium is where the real value of the house is concentrated. To come in under the contest's abnormally low cost ceiling, Roberts admits frankly, he designed a strictly functional model. For fancier shows and private clients, he simply puts more house behind the same basic solar unit. A few thousand dollars beyond the Cotati limit will pur-chase a house with another bedroom and a loftier, more impressive roofline.

Prefabrication contributed to cost-effectiveness in the house proper as well as in the solarium. Again, time and money for research and development were spent to make the prefab truly feasible. In this case, the walls are factory-made in four by eight foot units that are easily and quickly erected at the site. The factory can vary materials to give homeowners a choice of interior finish (wallpaper, wood paneling, textured sheetrock).

Instead of stud construction, the structure of these walls is post-and-beam. This is a historically

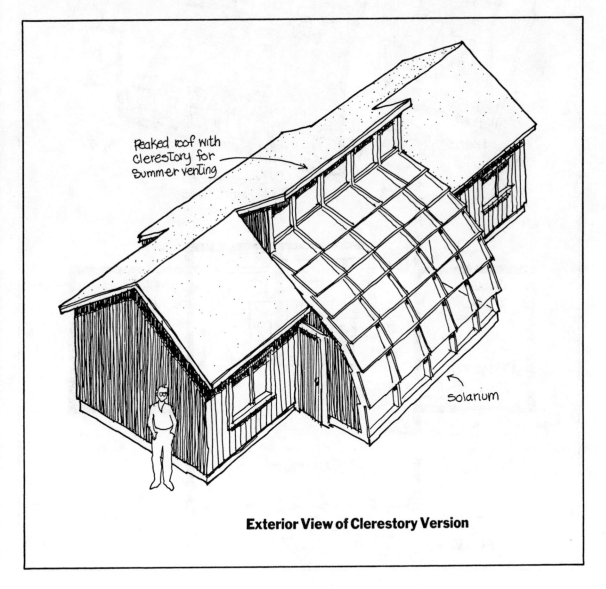

Peaked roof with clerestory for summer venting

solarium

Exterior View of Clerestory Version

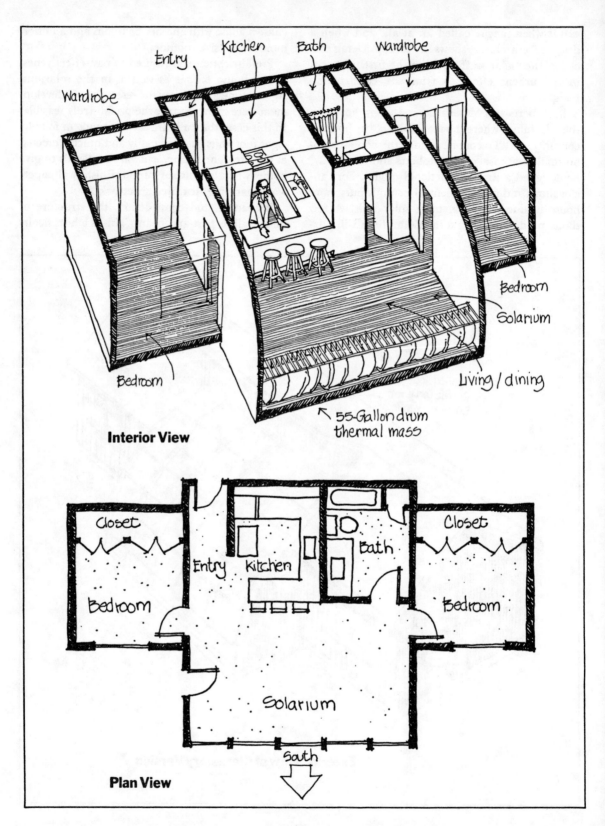

Entry

Kitchen

Bath

Wardrobe

Wardrobe

Bedroom

Bedroom

Solarium

55-Gallon drum thermal mass

Living / dining

Interior View

Closet

Closet

Entry

Kitchen

Bath

Bedroom

Bedroom

Solarium

South

Plan View

older and often stronger framing method that concentrates the load-bearing strength of the wall in fewer, bigger members (posts). The placement of the four by four posts every forty-eight inches along the perimeter (anchored in the concrete slab) eliminates all standard two by four stud construction. The four feet between posts is then free to receive the prefab walls, which are a pressed sandwich of exterior plywood, rigid polyurethane insulation, a vapor barrier, and sheetrock. Depending upon specific location and local requirements, the insulating panels can be built to have an R factor ranging from 13.5 to 36. Because the plywood, insulation, and sheetrock themselves are manufactured in four by eight foot sheets, there is no waste having to cut them to fit between or over studs. Because the insulation is solid, the entire wall is rigid and will not miss the bracing the studs provide.

The posts are eight feet high — also standard — but are cut unconventionally to receive the prefab walls: each post is a T with the crosspiece facing in. The tongue-and-groove exterior plywood of adjacent wall panels fits snugly over the base of the T, while the rest of the material stops at the T's stem. The clean and handsome effect for the occupant is one of exposed posts. Since the ceiling design calls for exposed beams (horizontal members which rest on the posts and tie the structure together), the total effect is one of exposed wooden arches.

Roberts believes that cutting the posts at the factory will go much faster than it would at a building site. Assembly lines and other factory equipment and routines streamline construction processes. There can be automation and work done to more precise specifications than in the field. Most significantly, the labor cost is much

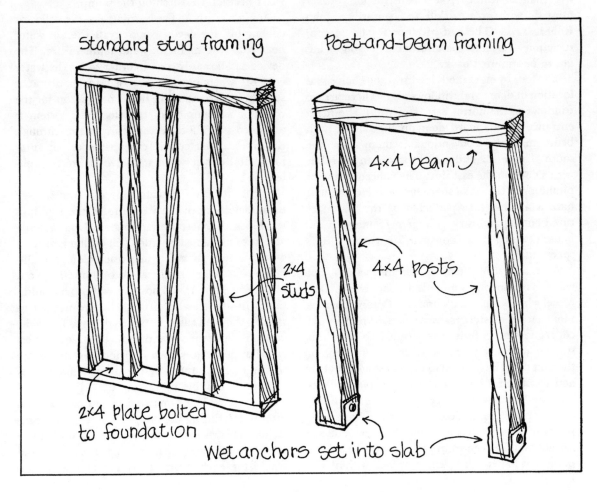

Standard stud framing   Post-and-beam framing

4×4 beam ↰

2×4 studs

4×4 posts

2×4 plate bolted to foundation

Wet anchors set into slab

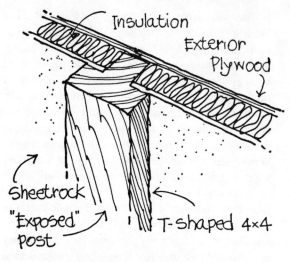

Prefabricated 4×4 Post

less because the work is simpler and more repetitive than what the typical construction worker must do with greater skill and versatility. John Roberts says, "The cost of labor for house construction — certainly for 'affordable housing' — has got to be trimmed back."

The four by eight modules direct the choice and location of doors and windows also. There are no windows on the north, east, and west. The main entrance is a standard door on the north. Both bedrooms have conventional windows on the south. The vertical sides of the solarium are solid, with a door on the east side. The concentration of plumbing in the small space between kitchen and bath is another idea perfected by the manufactured housing industry. A large percentage of the house's wiring runs conveniently through this space, too.

As in several of the other winning designs, hot water is developed by more than one source. Don Moser's heat gain calculations for Cotati convince him that an entirely transparent solarium would collect far more Btus than needed to heat this small house. He figured therefore that a section of the unit could be devoted to (and so shaded by) an active system for hot water. Two flat-plate collectors are built near the center of the solarium. They replace the highest, most nearly horizontal panes of glass at that location and consequently cannot even be seen from ground level outside, a point that Moser thinks will score well with neigh-

bors and passersby. The collectors are set directly into the beam support system, not attached above other structural members.

It's a short run of pipe from the top of these collectors to a specially designed 82-gallon hot water heater located in the pantry area. A heat exchanger in the woodstove pipe also develops hot water when a fire is burning and stores it in the tank. Controlling the hot water system is an electronic device which, by sensing the water temperature in the collector and the tank, decides when to run and when to stop a pump that draws hot water from collector to tank. (Because this is not a thermosiphon system, heated water will not flow on its own, so a pump is necessary.) The heat exchanger is not automatically operated because, unlike the collector, the stove operates at irregular hours; but hot water delivered by the exchanger influences the tank temperature and thus the device's decision to switch on the pump.

At night, with no fire burning and the collector cooling off, the device can activate the hot water heater itself to maintain water temperature. The device can be easily reset in order to let the water cool off when it won't be used for hours at a stretch. Two methods of freeze prevention for the collector are employed: the electronic system is activated at 38°F to recycle warm water through the pipes; under certain circumstances, an automatic draindown system will solve the freeze problem.

Except for the flat-plate collectors and storage drums, nothing in the structure of the solarium will block all that south-facing glass. Once again a variety of movable insulation will do the job. It's a set of shutters that slide in a track along the glulam beams. When not in use these shutters are out of sight in an overhead position and provide additional insulation above; when they're needed as shades, they can easily be pulled down as far as the counter above the water drums. Because a different shutter services each four-foot section of the solarium, fine tuning of the desired amount of sunlight is possible by varying the adjustment of each shutter. The same devices are called upon after sunset during the heating season to put insulation between living space and glass wall. (The intricacy of the system of angled notches and tracks for each beam easily explains why Don

Moser required months to perfect a master design and smooth operation.) To complete the insulating scheme, hinged insulated shutters cover the conventional windows.

Even with all the shades down on a hot day, warm air inside the house needs a way to be exhausted to the outside. This is handled with transom-type vents located at the top of the solarium on its north side, above the roof. A pole with a hook on one end is the simple tool for operating these vents, which are of insulating materials like those used in the solarium window shutters. (John Roberts looks forward to technological advances that will make automatic operation of the vents by photovoltaic cells cheaper.)

The designers anticipate that natural light will provide most of the light during the day. It's possible that this house will occasionally depend on electric lighting during the daytime if all the movable insulation is totally blocking out an intense afternoon sun. This would be quite a rare day in Cotati, however.

It's notable that Roberts and Moser plan a minor challenge to the prevailing building code. Regulations call for electrical outlets within six feet of every corner and no more than twelve feet apart along a wall. But in the small bedrooms of the solarium house, they think living up to the letter of that law goes beyond the occupants' predictable needs and thus adds unnecessary cost.

In contrast to the solarium itself, the rest of the Roberts/Moser design is flat-roofed. To ensure runoff of precipitation, polyurethane insulation is built up in an incline above the sheets of plywood which face into the house as its ceiling. This incline has a pitch of a quarter-inch per foot, sufficient for runoff. Around its perimeter, fascia (facing) boards retain the appearance of a flat roof. The insulation is covered with coats of a water-repellent liquid to finish the roofing.

Chapter Eight
The Gangnail House

Judges of the Cotati contest awarded first place to the design of Bruce Johnson, a San Francisco architect with a mission. He'd like to do nothing less than change the way most American houses are put together, and his design illustrates the imaginative and practical methods he proposes for the change.

At the heart of his system is a method of framing that equals or outperforms stick-built construction in strength, ease, time, and cost. Less material is wasted in the process and there's more flexibility in design. Pressed to fit his system into existing categories, Johnson labeled it a "modified post-and-beam," but he's rightfully proud of a system that is as promising as it is innovative.

Veteran builders will tell you there's nothing new under the sun, and Johnson freely acknowledges his borrowings from and adaptations of existing construction systems. The central element here is the method of fastening adjacent boards, a technique picked up from truss manufacturers. Factories are equipped with hydraulic presses in which boards are joined by gangnailing, a far stronger process than conventional nailing.

Gangnails are made in numerous sizes; Johnson uses a four by six inch sheet-metal plate which has been punched to create a "gang" of several hundred spikes in a close grid on one side. The spikes are only about a quarter-inch long, but when the plate is pressed into wood under 100 tons of pressure, they clench the wood fibers rather than separate them as nails do. The press forces the plate down until the top surface of the plate is flush with the surface of the wood. This technique gives wood the strength of steel and gives to each joint a rigidity that can't be achieved conventionally without additional bracing.

Picture four two by sixes formed into a rectangle. At each joint the boards merely butt against each other—no special milling or trimming needed here. They're gangnailed on both sides, the metal plate straddling the line where boards meet. The finished rectangle—Johnson calls it a frame—is the basic structural unit of an infinite number of possible designs. It is only one board wide (a "two by four" is actually only 1½ inches in that dimension) but is all the framing needed for a section or entire length of wall.

Now picture an assembly of four of these frames in a three-dimensional space. Where two frames meet in a corner, Johnson adds a jamb, a post to which both frames are nailed in addition to being nailed to each other. This is the basis for an entire room. Structurally it's finished, a cube or rectangular solid that is fully rigid in every direction.

Now, Johnson says, let your imagination go to work. These assemblies of frames can be of any size (twelve by twelve by eight feet high is typical), and they can be joined and stacked to create all sorts of floor plans, elevations, and design possibilities. It's a modular system, but each module can conceivably be a different size.

At his small two-man plant in South San Francisco, the architect/builder fashions only the flat frames; but, having conceived the house as composed entirely of these frames, he can fabricate every one of them in the hydraulic press. The entire requirement of frames, each just one board thick, can then be stacked on the back of one truck and shipped to a building site.

A simple foundation method has already been followed at the site. At the points where posts will stand, a two-foot hole is dug; sand is put in the bottom; and a preformed sixteen by eighteen inch concrete slab is set on the sand. On top of the slab stands a concrete cylinder with a specially made

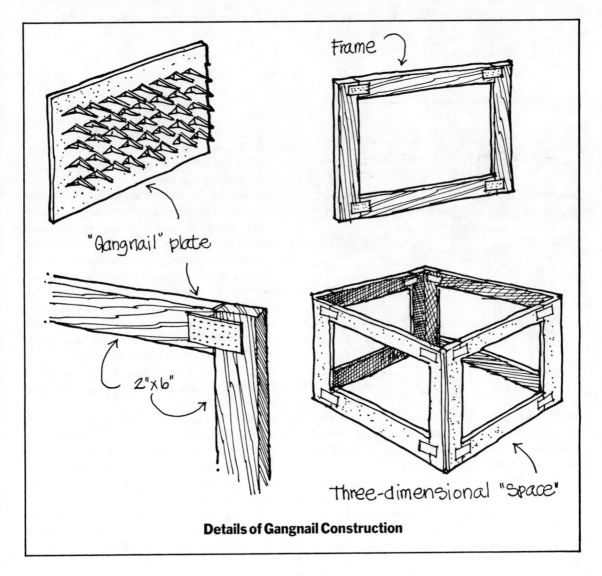

"Gangnail" plate

Frame

2"x6"

three-dimensional "space"

Details of Gangnail Construction

The Gangnail House

DESIGNER:	Bruce Johnson
AREA:	643 square feet, including 150 square feet (loft)
FLOOR PLAN:	two bedrooms on first floor, bathroom at landing, third bedroom and open loft above
FOUNDATION TYPE:	pier and post
CONSTRUCTION TYPE:	modified post-and-beam, prefabricated framing system
PASSIVE-SOLAR FEATURES:	*space heat:* thermal chimney, brick floor as thermal mass; *water heat:* breadbox; *other:* thermal-mass chamber below floor
BACKUP SYSTEMS:	woodburning stove; gas water heater; reversible, variable-speed fan
OTHER FEATURES:	200-square-foot deck, small covered entrance deck, storage cabinets on outside wall

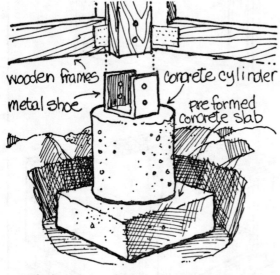

wooden frames metal shoe concrete cylinder preformed concrete slab

metal shoe on top; the wooden members that comprise the post fit snugly inside the shoe — and framing can proceed. Later the hole is backfilled with more concrete and soil.

One of several advantages of this pier-and-post type of foundation is that it works on uneven ground and on remote sites that heavy earthmoving equipment can't reach. (Many property owners want to disturb their building site as little as possible.) If necessary, each post can rise a different height from the ground in order to support a floor that comes out level.

Assembly of the flat frames takes place at the site and thus is accomplished by conventional nailing. In forming the posts, the wood members are sometimes joined also by bolts. With the first-story assemblies complete, joists are nailed to the frames to support the floor. Where the house will be two stories, the jambs run the entire height up from the foundation and are ready to receive the upper-level frames. Frame by frame, the wall structure of the whole house is rapidly assembled. From the tops of the frames, rafters are raised to receive the roof. Second-story frame assemblies can also be put together on the ground and lifted into place by a crane.

Johnson describes his framing system as "completely abnormal" for a building process. The assembly of a cube takes about twenty minutes. A typical small house, such as this Cotati winner, is made up of about forty of these units. The labor involved here is quite simple and repetitive; a color coding system eliminates mistakes. Significantly, this work requires an "assembler" rather than a carpenter. A fair wage for an assembler

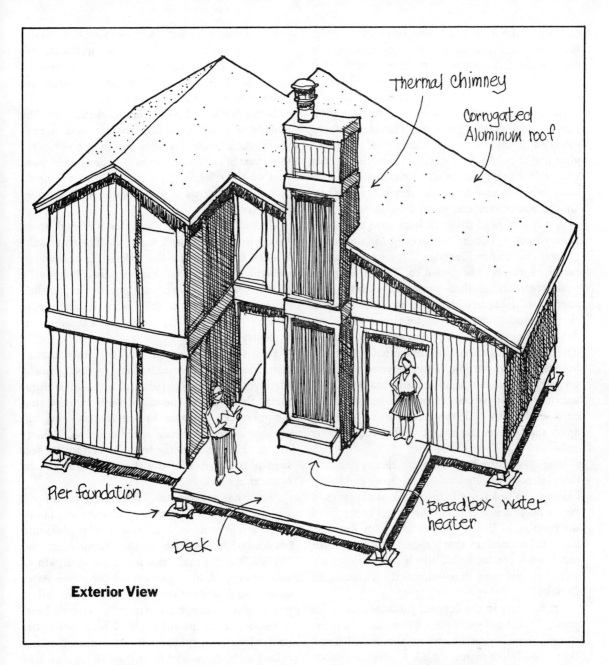

thermal chimney

Corrugated Aluminum roof

Pier foundation

Deck

Breadbox water heater

Exterior View

may be half of a union carpenter's wage or less, and the number of assembler-hours per house is limited by the ease with which the units go together. Johnson has successfully built houses this way with a crew of three "kids just out of high school."

The earlier history of his framing system lay in Johnson's long experience in designing and building vacation cabins. Here the need is for a building that can be put up fairly quickly and finished in one summer so that it is secure over the winter and ready to be enjoyed the next summer. Usually the building sites for such cabins are not level; often they are remote. The owners nearly always desire a small house, a simple shelter in which, Johnson says, they can "get away from all the things and drudgeries that are hanging around our heads" in the rest-of-the-year house. They are happy to reduce the number and level of amenities, and usually they are interested in flexible, vigorous designs that might cause too much stir in the city. All this created a design experience that prepared Johnson remarkably well for the Cotati contest.

In one cabin, the owner decided to have glass surround the entire first floor. This requirement matched Johnson's own fondness for plenty of glass and could be successfully accomplished only with a framing system that eliminates, as Johnson's does, the need for studs every sixteen inches. Of course, not everyone wants all-glass walls, and to satisfy this need studs go back into the space between posts. They're not needed for structural purposes but to provide something for interior and exterior surfaces to be nailed to. This is a significant compromise that somewhat dilutes the strength of Johnson's idea. But the fact remains that the studs don't *have* to be there; so sliding doors and very large windows can be accommodated nearly anywhere they're wanted (especially for passive-solar purposes), and recycled and odd-shaped windows can be hung individually without worrying about reducing a wall's strength. Even on a windowless wall, the studs can be two feet apart rather than the sixteen inches required by code.

Johnson's frame assemblies are clearly compatible with prefabricated walls (and floors and roofs) like the ones described in the previous chapter. In fact, a notable side effect of the Cotati contest was the meeting of Bruce Johnson and John Roberts. Some hybrid designs that utilize ideas from both men's work are being built in a subdivision they and their partners have launched. (It too is in Cotati.)

For his entry in the contest, Johnson planned a passive-solar house of a total 643 square feet, including three bedrooms, two on the second floor. One of the latter rooms is a loft which looks down onto the living room.

For all the modernity of his technical ideas, the architect is a conservative in his attitudes about living space. He is quite critical of open floor plans, strongly preferring that each room be defined and closed off from the others for privacy and soundproofing. Thus the kitchen is separated from the dining room by a sliding panel and two of the bedrooms are fully private units. Out of a personal dislike for bathrooms located immediately off living areas, he placed the bathroom for this house off the stair landing, halfway between the two floors. Toilet and bathing/dressing areas are separated, each with its own door.

Beneath the bathroom and accessible from the outside only are a laundry room and a storage room. All of these facilities are on the northernmost part of the house, repeating the good ideas of putting these less often used areas on the north and reinforcing their buffer value with outside-only access.

Under the upper flight of stairs is enough room for the refrigerator and a pantry. The rest of the kitchen appliances are lined along the north wall; with the bathroom and laundry fixtures physically (but not visually or audibly) nearby, a prefabricated plumbing tree in the "wet wall" can supply (and vent) sinks, toilet, washer, and shower conveniently.

Even though his design calls for more interior partitions to define individual rooms, Johnson manages to reduce circulation areas to a minimum; this is one of the major ways, he says, that designers can decrease square footage and still give the occupant living space and value. Entry into the house is from the west. Fifteen square feet here plus the area of the stairs is about all the space that's strictly for traffic.

"Solar has got to come," Johnson notes simply, and he assists the process by working some familiar as well as some unusual passive-solar ideas into his design. A brick floor in the dining room and kitchen is a thermal mass for the direct gain of solar energy. A forty-gallon breadbox-type water heater sits outside at the base of the south wall; it preheats the water in a thirty-gallon electric heater located in the laundry room. The breadbox has an insulated, hinged cover which, when open, is a reflector. Window and door glass is concentrated on the south and eliminated on the north.

The "thermal chimney" that rises the entire height of the south wall and above it requires detailed examination. On its south face, double-pane glass is separated by a half-inch air space from a wall made of muffin tins! Very cheap stamped-aluminum TV-dinner plates, or actual muffin tins, are what Johnson in fact proposes to use for this solar collector surface. The extensive

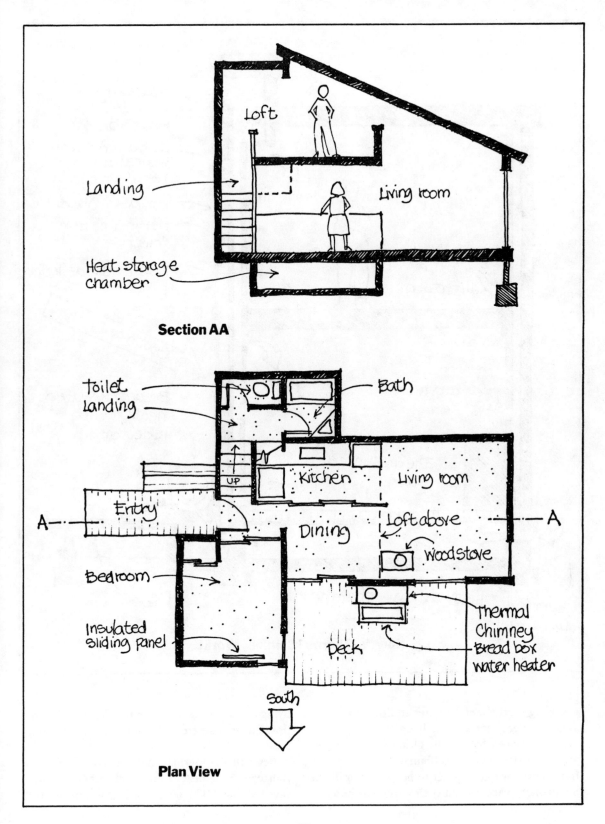

Section AA

Loft

Landing

Living room

Heat storage chamber

Plan View

toilet
landing

Bath

Entry

UP

Kitchen

Living room

A · — · — · —

Loft above

— · — · A

Dining

Wood stove

Bedroom

Insulated sliding panel

Deck

thermal
chimney
Bread box
water heater

South

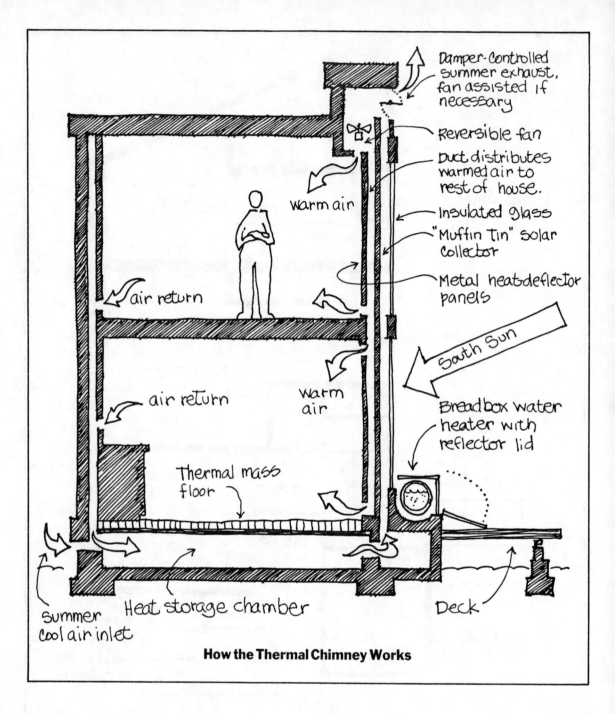

How the Thermal Chimney Works

wrinkling on the metal creates additional surface area to reflect heat and stir it up.

Heat, trapped behind the glass, will rise in the air space to the top of the chimney and be directed from there, by a fan, either to bedrooms or down a four-inch space behind the muffin tins into the living areas. Rising hot air in the thermal chimney draws in cool air from the house at the chimney's base.

Beneath the thermal mass floor is an eight by fourteen foot heat storage chamber—another thermal mass. The heat that it stores moves to it not directly, from the sun, but indirectly from heat sources within the structure. Basically this is a big shallow concrete box that occupies all the space between the floor and the soil. It's insulated on the sides and bottom, rests on a layer of sand, and can be filled with rocks, concrete blocks, water-filled bottles, a waterbed mattress, or some other dense heat storage material.

Fan-forced hot air from the thermal chimney passes through this chamber. Cooler air in the house can also sink out of the living areas, through vents, into it. Because the brick floor is at the top of the chamber, some of its heat capacity will affect the warm air storage in the chamber, too. Together these inputs will store heat in the storage material, which, like the floor, will give up heat at night.

The interior layers of the thermal chimney include, besides the four-inch air space, plywood with foil-faced insulation and decorative metal heat-deflector panels. Insulation is needed to protect the plywood from the intense heat generated in the collector. The heat-deflector panels face into the living room, where they can increase the heating job done by a woodburning stove. Heat from the stove will also contribute to the amount being stored in the thermal masses.

Johnson says he has always liked woodburning stoves and makes a simple but telling point about them. "You need a place to burn all the paper and cardboard that piles up. Why not do that and get warm at the same time?" Once again the stovepipe rises entirely within the two floors of living space.

During the cooling cycle, the hot air developed in the thermal chimney, instead of being routed into the house, is simply vented to the outside at the top of the chimney. The fan is reversible and runs at variable speeds, so if necessary it can help pull air up and out. This upward draw of warm air, fan-aided or not, induces movement in the entire volume of air in the house. The storage chamber has air intakes that can be opened in summer, thus allowing the cool air under the house and on the north to feed into the ventilation system.

All the fixed glass in the house is the double-pane type. Johnson likes to combine a tall fixed-glass window (all the way to the ceiling) with a small openable window beneath it to aid ventila-tion. There's a skylight set into the bathroom ceiling. Drapes and sliding insulated shutters cover windows on the inside.

Walls in the gangnail house could be installed quickly; Johnson would preassemble panels of various lengths with plywood exterior, gypsum board interior, and R-11 rolled insulation between. He appreciates the virtues of insulation and points out the contribution it makes toward soundproofing, but he's skeptical about recent trends toward thicker walls. He says, "The extra air space in them is not for additional insulation value — it's to keep the insulation dry." Where the warm air mass inside a house meets the cold air mass outside, there's got to be some condensation. In a poor wall design the insulation ends up behaving like a sponge and giving up its intended function.

Because the wall panels in this design are slightly thicker than the structural frames, they provide a "raceway" for wires. This means that most of the wall panels can be assembled without concern for wiring. Johnson is convinced that electrical codes call for more amperage than we need and more outlets than we use. Like many other critics of conventional building practice, he believes that such code requirements reflect the interests of the producers more than those of consumers of electricity.

The considerable savings he projected from the use of his framing system and other ideas left room even in the tight Cotati budget for a seven by sixteen foot sun deck on the south. Much of the glass on the south wall is in the form of sliding doors, which open onto the deck. The breadbox rests on the deck and part of the heat storage chamber lies beneath it. Another smaller deck extends out from the west entry. This deck will be covered by a low roof projection, a much appreciated amenity during wet weather as well as a summer source of shade. The deck is two steps above ground level, making storage space beneath.

More than the rest of the winners this one achieves an angular layout that is visually interesting and somehow appears spacious even while it is compact. Again, the easy joining and stacking of modules made this effect possible at low cost.

The roofline is quite varied, dominated by the towering thermal chimney and breaking at several

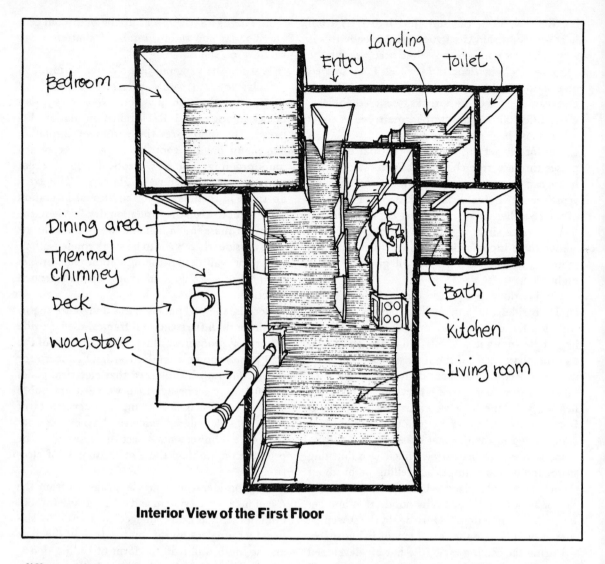

Bedroom

Entry

Landing

Toilet

Dining area

Thermal chimney

Deck

Woodstove

Bath

Kitchen

Living room

Interior View of the First Floor

different pitches. It appears quite modern but without an excessively solar look. Another of the architect's preferences is demonstrated on the roof, where corrugated aluminum is the exterior surface. He's convinced that the metal roof "gives more for your money": it's fire retardant; when coated with a tar derivative it doesn't look shiny (asphalt shingles are a far greater drain on oil resources than this coating is); it reflects the sun (unusable or unwanted heat gain); and, with the ridges and furrows that many brands offer, it creates an air flow that dissipates heat faster than other roofing materials.

The design's angularity also identifies several obvious places for expansion and further develop-

ment. Johnson envisions a covered carport on the northwest; under it a car could park quite close to the entry. The area along the north wall could be a patio; or the storage space, which presently opens onto it, could be enlarged into a workroom. The raised floor level and pier foundation system would make it easy to add more decks. Opening up existing walls for room enlargement would be easier, too, because the nonbearing studs and panels could be removed without need for special temporary bracing and permanent structural rebuilding.

Bruce Johnson took a major role in designing the site plan too, the layout of the houses on the property selected and bought for the project by

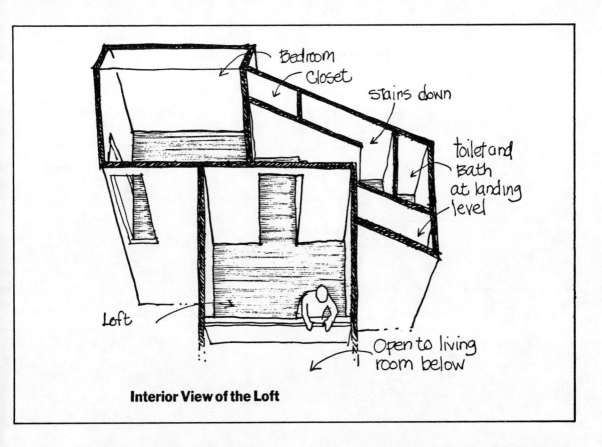

Bedroom
Closet

Stairs down

toilet and
Bath
at landing
level

Loft

Open to living
room below

Interior View of the Loft

the City of Cotati. In the jargon of city planners, the project is a PUD (planned unit development), a variety of subdivision which Johnson would like to see employed more widely. While many tracts of new housing are unimaginative grids of straight streets with the separate houses all squarely facing the streets, the PUD allows the houses to be both clustered and individually oriented.

Clustering allows a higher than normal density (units per acre) in exchange for some land in the development remaining as open space or recreational areas owned in common by all the homeowners. Clustering tends to reduce the amount of road needed — valuable space that can be used for something besides paving. Shorter underground water, electricity, and sewage lines are required, too, when the units aren't so far apart. That makes those services cheaper to install. Individual orientation means above all that solar houses can face the sun instead of the street. Existing trees and shrubs can be usefully incorporated into the solar designs. Greater freedom of orientation also means that site planners can create flexible and livable combinations that maintain individual privacy while encouraging community sharing and interaction.

Part Three
Beyond Design

Chapter Nine
A Solar Primer for Homeowners: Conclusion

Many more passive-solar principles and numerous ways of applying them can be found outside the scope of the Cotati contest. Some of these are presented in this chapter, not in the context of complete designs for a house, but as a miscellany of good ideas that can bring down the cost of owning and operating a home.

CLERESTORIES

Clerestories are small windows located high on a building's profile. They admit light to the upper portions of a room; more significantly, in a passive-solar design they are often placed so that they allow solar radiation to strike a thermal mass in the *northern* interior. The roof of a building can

be planned so that the clerestories are not on the southernmost wall but closer to the middle of the building, on the short plane connecting two different slopes. In this position they allow the sun to penetrate further to the north.

Clerestories open lots of possibilities. The thermal mass need not be positioned on the south side of the house: it can be placed on the north side or be set in both places for additional heat capacity. This positioning helps distribute radiation more evenly through the house and makes the northern parts more than a barrier against heat loss and cold air infiltration. Clerestories also make the roofline more interesting than a single-slope roof (and more expensive) from outside and are pleasing light sources for the inside. Naturally, the in-

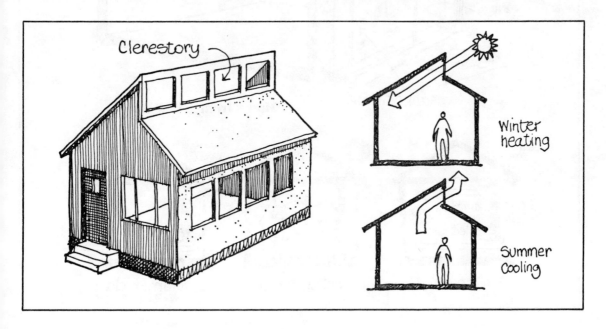

Clerestory

Winter heating

Summer cooling

terior design should cooperate with intent of the clerestory. For example, a loft floor should not block the rays entering through the clerestories from reaching the living spaces below.

Clerestories can be designed to open in order to facilitate ventilation. They can also be set up with reflectors, overhangs, and movable insulation.

TROMBE WALLS

A Trombe wall combines several passive-solar principles and makes it possible to collect heat without letting too much light enter through a south wall. This feature makes Trombe walls useful in design situations where, for example, the view to the south is undesirable or excessive daylight is regarded as a problem.

Named for its inventor, the French designer Felix Trombe, this device places a sheet of glass a few inches away from a dark-colored masonry wall. The wall is typically eight or more inches thick and functions as a thermal mass, slowly absorbing heat during the day for reradiation at night. But the greenhouse effect causes heat to build up in the air space between glass and wall much faster than the wall can absorb it. This surplus rises and passes into the living area behind the wall through vents at the top of the wall. The rising heat draws in cold air from the interior through vents near the floor, creating a convective loop.

At night during the heating cycle, the vents are closed and a curtain of insulation may be lowered in the air space between the wall and glass to re-

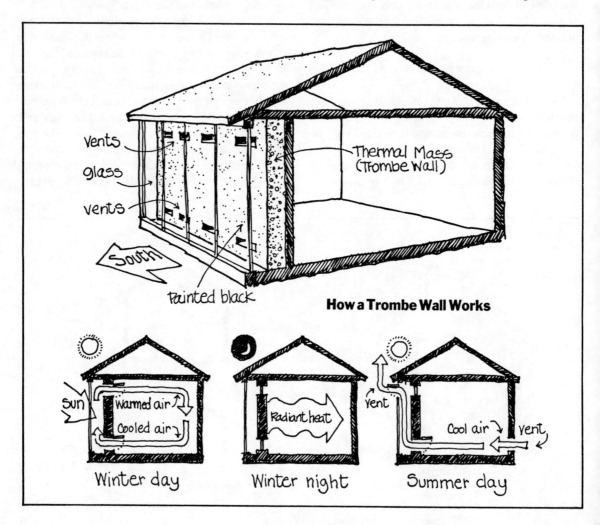

How a Trombe Wall Works

Winter day   Winter night   Summer day

duce heat loss and concentrate the reradiation toward the interior. The same curtain or an overhang can block the sun from reaching the wall in summer; exterior vents at the top of the glass wall exhaust heat to the outside. If necessary, small fans can be included to help move volumes of air in the desired direction.

Depending on factors presented by the specific location and design, Trombe walls can be modified in several ways. The thermal chimney in Bruce Johnson's design—the gangnail house—is based on similar principles. In other designs, instead of a few inches, the air space can be wide enough to form a sitting room where light and warmth can be enjoyed; here the Trombe wall's relation to solariums and attached greenhouses is evident. Deliberately wide spacing of a few bricks or concrete blocks in the wall, or additional vents, allows diffused light to enter the interior. These variations will affect the wall's performance and so must be included in thermal calculations.

The masonry is likely to be a load-bearing stretch of the south wall, but it doesn't have to be. As a freestanding thermal mass it can be treated as a decorative device and, especially when facing living areas, set to present appealing lines and textures.

PLANNING FOR TEMPERATURE FLUCTUATION

The Trombe wall is an example of an indirect-gain design. In these, the temperature in the collecting device can fluctuate much more than would be comfortable in a living space. Deliberate overheating here can actually contribute to cooling the rest of the house (discussed later in this chapter). Since direct-gain designs, such as using a concrete slab floor as thermal mass, admit light directly into living spaces, temperature fluctuation must be controlled much more strictly.

In planning for heat storage by direct gain in masonry thermal masses, we must keep certain concepts in mind. Masonry absorbs heat slowly, and intense sunlight on a small area is likely to increase room temperature while not significantly speeding the rate at which heat is absorbed by the storage mass. Less intense radiation over a larger surface moderates fluctuations in room temperature and stores more heat at the same time.

With the sunlight distributed widely over its surface, the storage mass—for direct gain—generally does not need to be more than four inches thick. If the design concentrates sunlight on less area, storage can be increased somewhat by increasing the mass's thickness, up to eight inches. Beyond that point, however, increasing thickness has no beneficial effect on heat storage efficiency.

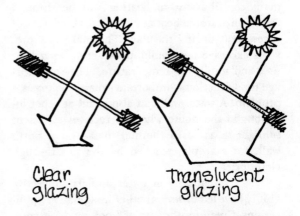

Clear glazing   Translucent glazing

Ways to distribute sunlight include using a number of small windows to admit it in patches; using light-colored interior nonstoring surfaces to reflect it to dark storage surfaces; not using wall-to-wall carpets on masonry floors. Translucent glazing scatters sunlight so that it is more evenly distributed over walls, ceiling, and floor. It reduces glare and maintains privacy. The need in direct-gain designs for considerable heat-storage area makes it sensible to distribute thermal masses around the room. Translucent glazing decreases the intensity of rays reaching a single surface but does not reduce the overall amount of solar energy entering the space. When skylights and clerestories admit light into a direct-gain design, they should be equipped with shading devices so that they don't contribute to overheating during mild and warm periods.

WATER WALLS AND ROOF PONDS

Water can be used instead of masonry to make up a heat storage wall. This will not be a load-bearing wall but a concentration of water behind a window in a regular wall. Water can be contained not only in metal drums but in sealed concrete or in translucent plastic structures that stand from floor to ceiling. The translucent arrangement allows some light to pass through it. Such a "water wall" is superior to masonry in that convection in the water distributes heat more rapidly throughout the wall. This wall is unlikely to be vented at top and bottom, however, in which case (unlike the Trombe wall) it won't allow circulation of hot air into the living area during the day. So its main contributions to heating will be through radiation of stored heat at night and absorption of excess heat during the day. Thermal mass prevents excessive heat buildup by acting as a heat sink and stabilizing temperature. The sink/storage dual function is important where cooling is a problem. A water wall can also stand at other locations in the house where it receives sufficient sunlight to act as a thermal mass—on a north wall, for example, reached by the sun through clerestories.

The heat capacity of water and its convective ability have led to several other imaginative applications. Credit for the idea of "roof ponds" is commonly given to Harold Hay of Atascadero, California. In his Skytherm house, Hay places water encased in large plastic bags on a roof that also serves as the ceiling of the living space below. Effective insulation is crucial: during the day, while the dark-colored bags absorb heat, insulating

Winter day

Winter night

Summer day

Summer night

panels are folded or slid aside; at night, they block heat loss to the sky and make the bags a source of radiant heat to the space below. To help with cooling, they're used in a reverse manner. Covered during the day, they absorb heat rising from the interior; uncovered at night, they release it to the sky.

With a roof pond, any room in a structure can have its own solar heater without having to face south. The roof is the most out-of-the-way location for solar devices. Of course, the extra weight of the bags and precipitation runoff from the flat roof must be planned for in the structure. The insulation scheme, moreover, probably needs to be mechanized.

Small plastic "pillows" are items manufactured to serve as portable water heaters. These dark-colored collectors can be permanently positioned on a roof and used to preheat an indoor hot water tank.

The Cool Pool idea of Jonathan Hammond and James Plumb of Winters, California, combines elements of the water wall and roof pond to achieve an efficient cooling system for a hot climate. In this design, tall water walls located near the middle of the floor plan connect to two horizontal pools on the roof. The walls absorb heat from the interior, and natural thermosiphoning causes the warm water to rise into the pools, where the heat is dissipated. Louvers over the pools block the sun but let warm air pass up and out. Cooler water drops into the walls to make the cycle continuous. No pumps or fans are involved; the only manual operation required is twice-a-year opening/closing the valves in the line between walls and pools to set the system for heating or cooling.

HOLDING THE HEAT

On cloudy days, passive-solar designs collect some energy but usually not enough to maintain a desired temperature. Sufficiently prolonged periods of cloudiness call for use of auxiliary heat, but houses can be designed to store heat for more than one night. Once again this is a matter of insulating the house well and then enlarging the area of glazing, the thickness of thermal mass, or both. Deliberate oversizing of this type can create overheating problems in some climates and situations

—it's a tradeoff. Given the ability of a woodstove to serve as an entirely satisfactory backup heater, and the fact that some stretches of weather each year are certain to render passive-solar heating insufficient, it may not be worth the expense and potential overheating to expand solar capacity very much. At such times the house's ability to hold onto heat is more important than its restricted ability to collect it—thus the importance of insulation.

Here again the basic climate of the region should be the guiding factor in the design. Where sunshine is abundant (even on cold days, as in New Mexico and Colorado) the design decision will be different than for places that get lots of cloudy weather (even though they remain mild, as in the Pacific Northwest and San Francisco Bay Area). In a sunny climate, a thick thermal mass may be justified for dealing with short periods of cloudiness, but a thick mass does not respond quickly to sunlight after many cloudy days and would be a poor choice in a cloudy region.

OPENERS AND CLOSERS

Various ways to open and close windows and to raise and lower shades are required by passive-solar designs. Every design calls for the user's participation to make heating and cooling systems work properly. Sometimes operable devices are located in clerestories or places that are hard to reach. Plenty of old ideas are gainfully employed solving these contemporary problems. Cord-and-pulley arrangements, crank-type mechanisms, pull chains and springs, and hooked poles all have their useful place.

An invention by solar pioneer Steve Baer lets lowered overhangs change position automatically. Freon responds to fluctuating temperatures by contracting and expanding. This response alternately forces louvers into more vertical or more horizontal positions. Automatic timers (such as thermostats) and light-sensitive devices can also operate the movable parts of passive-solar homes.

RETRACTABLE INSULATION

One of the most ingenious devices in all of solar technology is a special kind of movable insulation.

In this case, a narrow air space is alternately filled with and emptied of very small polyurethane beads. Pumped in, this Beadwall (also a Steve Baer invention) packs into dense efficient insulation; vacuumed out, the window is free to collect solar energy. The dependence on a small motor to operate this device makes it both more convenient and more expensive than insulating shades.

For designs that call for unfurling some material during the cooling cycle, exterior shades are superior to interior ones. By keeping the sun's rays from reaching glass in the first place, they eliminate the heat buildup that would occur between the glass and an interior shade. That heat has to be vented somewhere and its intensity may damage certain shade materials.

REFLECTORS

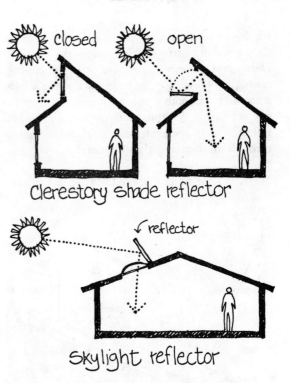

Clerestory shade reflector

Skylight reflector

Reflectors have been mentioned in connection with breadbox water heaters. They can also increase the amount of sun collected by other passive devices. The remote location of clerestories may create an area on the roof where reflectors that boost the amount of light entering these windows aren't visible. Exterior insulating shades for

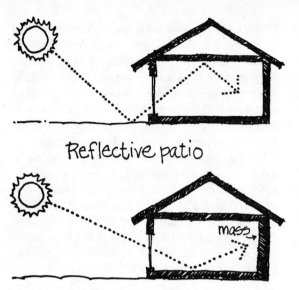

Reflective patio

Reflective floor

windows can double as reflectors if, when open, they are shiny surfaces lying below the window. Here again, numerous means of opening, closing, raising, and lowering can be used. Putting a light color and a smooth finish on a concrete patio is one way to make this multiuse area a helpful reflector that bounces additional solar energy through south-facing glass in winter.

FLAT-PLATE COLLECTORS

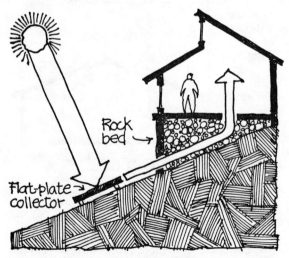

Space heating using thermosiphon flat-plate solar collector

Flat-plate collectors (see Chapter Four) can be used to supply warm air as well as to heat water for domestic use. Using either air or water as a medium for heat transfer, the collector can be placed away from the house (down a slight slope, for example) or at the base of a wall. From this position thermosiphoning carries the medium heated in the collector up to a storage chamber. If the transfer medium is air, the storage chamber is usually filled with rocks to absorb the heat. The cooled air drops to the bottom of the chamber and down through ducts to the collector for reheating. If the transfer medium is water, the storage chamber is a water tank. Either way, while the sun shines heat is being stored. Pumps and fans add possibilities for moving greater volumes of heat over greater distance, but good design can create an efficient system that's entirely passive.

COOLING THE HOUSE

The direction of prevailing summer winds is important information for designing efficient methods of cooling the house. As a general rule, put high vents and openable windows on the leeward side (away from the wind) to let the hottest air escape. Windows and low vents on the windward

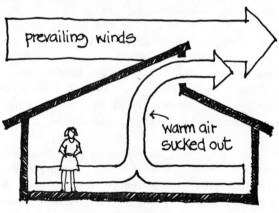

Venting

side admit cooler air to replace the hot air. Making leeward openings substantially larger than windward ones achieves optimal cooling rates by increasing the draw of cooler air. Wind turbine vents at or near the roof peak also enhance air flow and improve the cooling rate; so do upward drafts created by the slope of the roof.

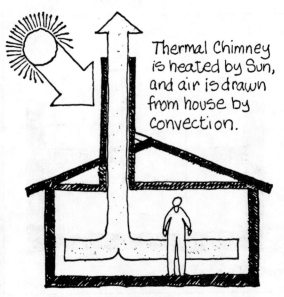

Thermal Chimney is heated by Sun, and air is drawn from house by convection.

Thermal Chimney

A factor in the mathematical formula for determining cooling rates is the difference in air temperature between escaping indoor air and entering outdoor air. By deliberately raising the temperature of the former, a more rapid cooling flow is induced. A Trombe wall operating in the summer, for example, will develop very hot air (above 150°F), which rises quickly; its escape to the outside draws more cool air into the house from the north and through the lower vent in the Trombe wall. Some thermal chimney designs employ fixed glass and heat-absorbing materials near the top for deliberate overheating.

One way to procure the coolest possible air without mechanical refrigeration is to introduce it through long tubes buried in the ground. Despite warm surface temperatures, earth several feet down remains cool; warm outdoor air entering the tube cools substantially before entering the house. Simple techniques will keep these tubes free of rodents, water, or dirt, which could block the passage of air.

The virtues of earth are numerous in contributing to passive-solar heating and cooling. Above all, earth's steadiness of temperature makes it a good shield from fluctuating conditions in the air. Designs for underground houses rely on this property to sustain remarkably even maximum and minimum temperatures. In conventional designs, particularly on sites with even a slight slope, earth berms can shelter foundations and parts of walls from cold winds and temperatures.

Sloped designs sometimes incorporate earth as roofing material for a partially underground design. A few innovators use sod on the roofs of fully aboveground structures. Unlike most roofing materials, which shed water, earth absorbs it. This capacity means that such houses can use evaporative cooling methods. When water absorbs a large amount of heat from its surroundings, it evaporates. This principle is familiar in the cooling effect of perspiration evaporating from the human skin; on a dry, hot day, body temperature is partially controlled by this rapid evaporation. Similarly, water held by soil on a roof can absorb heat rising from the interior and dissipate it as the

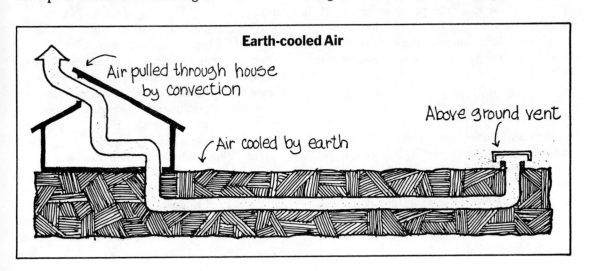

Earth-cooled Air

Air pulled through house by convection

Air cooled by earth

Above ground vent

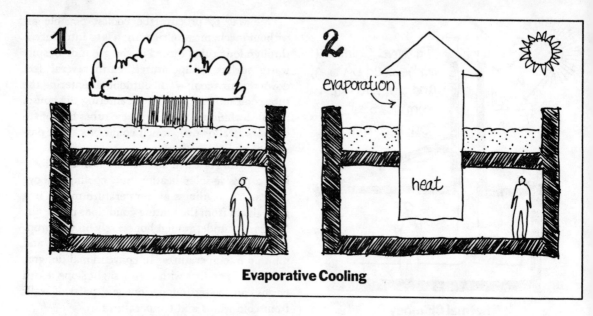

Evaporative Cooling

water evaporates. Rooftop sprinklers on conventional roofs get similar results. Applications like these are best suited to climates where cooling is the main design problem to be solved.

PRECAST CONCRETE

Precast concrete walls, which are being used increasingly in house construction, have important applications for passive-solar performance. Precasting is performed at the site: concrete is poured in a mold on the ground and allowed to set; then the wall is tilted into place. Insulated with urethane and finished with stucco (optional), this substantial thermal mass performs better in this regard than the wood frame it replaces. Gaining additional thermal mass in the walls yields an advantage in terms of temperature fluctuation control.

FANS

Fans can be used to move warm air into storage as well as out of the house for ventilation. Warm air collected inside a clerestory, for example, can be forced down a hollow core to be absorbed by interior concrete-block walls that don't receive sunlight directly. In this way more of the house can be used for thermal mass without having to design bigger windows.

SUPERINSULATION

Somewhat in contrast to the passive-solar methods of storing heat, "superinsulated" houses concentrate on stopping heat loss. While these designs utilize principles of solar orientation, they do not deliberately add thermal mass: the mass of the house itself is regarded as sufficient. Thick insulation is applied not only to walls but also to sills, headers, window frames, and foundation walls. A plastic vapor-barrier sheet applied to the inner faces of all external walls and ceilings stops infiltration and prevents the buildup of moisture within the insulation. The windows are double or triple glazed.

In such a house, a significant amount of heat is supplied by human bodies, light bulbs, cooking stoves, and other appliances. Moderate-size south windows gather some solar radiation, which the house holds as heat. Portable heaters are sufficient to supply the additional heat needed — there is no need for furnace, oil tank, radiators, or any other element of central heating systems.

The "Illinois Lo-Cal House," designed by the Small Homes Council-Building Research Council at the University of Illinois, is a carefully tested model of such a house. The researchers state that this house uses approximately one-third of the energy needed to heat a house of the same size (approximately 1,500 square feet) built to meet

1974 insulation standards for the cold climate of the Midwest.

Although the Illinois Lo-Cal House is wholly conventional in appearance, one of several innovative construction details is the double-framed wall. Staggered studs within this extra-thick (8½ inches) wall allow insulation to be thicker and continuous; such insulation is an improvement over the interruption caused by the studs in a conventional wall, which allows greater infiltration.

The exceptional tightness of the superinsulated house disturbs some critics, who suggest there may be problems of buildup of moisture, pollutants, and stale air inside. But its proponents say this house can breathe too — if necessary, with air-to-air exchanger devices that transfer heat from the air being exhausted to the air being drawn in from outside. Leading solar researcher William Shurcliff predicts that superinsulated houses will soon emerge as the design providing the greatest comfort for the smallest overall costs (construction plus operating costs) and that they will come to be the norm against which various other designs can be usefully measured.

insulation   studs

staggered studs provide more room for insulation.

sheetrock

staggered studs

Chapter Ten
Other Paths Toward
The Affordable House

There are many other paths to follow and points to consider on the way to finding and living in an affordable home of your own. This chapter surveys some of these other directions to make you aware of options that lie beyond the relatively narrow range of the Cotati designs.

THE PACKAGED HOUSE

A major trend in the housing industry is the increased availability of a wide variety of products that can all be labeled manufactured housing: log and timber homes, domes and yurts, panelized, precut, or modular house kits, mobile homes, and more. All of these types are basically designed by the manufacturers. However, some manufacturers say they rarely create two identical houses; in other words, the buyer makes so many specific choices that each house is different. The manufacturer offers stock models, as few as three or more than a hundred, but allows room for modifications to all of them.

Building houses in factories is an approach with several inherent advantages over site-built housing, and these attract increasing attention to this industry. Mass purchasing power yields cost savings on materials. Automated processes minimize waste of material and time lost in manually fitting pieces together. Vandalism and theft are greatly reduced. Ample inventories avoid work stoppages.

Work often must stop at a building site during inclement weather. In a factory, building can proceed day and night. And while factory workers may earn less than half what union craftsmen do per hour, they may also end the year with more total income because their pay has been much steadier.

Manufactured houses, in the form of kits, prefabricated panels, or fully finished sections, are delivered by truck to a house site that has been prepared independently. Site preparation and foundation are usually the owner's separate responsibility. Foundation types are conventional; the various manufactured houses can be placed on a full basement, a concrete-walled crawl space, a concrete slab, or an arrangement of piers.

To suit particular site, climate, and design requirements — passive solar, for example — the buyer may want a particular foundation type. This decision in turn influences the decision to buy a particular manufactured house, although many models can be built up from a variety of foundations. What the delivered package will include is again a matter of wide variety. It may be only precut boards or logs, or everything you need to complete construction. Everything you have to buy elsewhere is of course part of the total cost of the finished house.

All this variety is really the point with manufactured housing. The choices exist so that buyers can be involved and get the house they want at the price they've determined they can afford. The variety can lead to confusion, though. Terminology, for example, is something of a problem when it comes to classifying and describing manufactured housing. Manufacturers' names and their self-descriptions aren't entirely consistent and words like "precut," "modular," "kit," and "log" are used without much precision.

LOG AND TIMBER HOUSES

Log and timber house packages usually consist of a basic shell—the walls and roof. The wood members have been precut and assembly is reasonably straightforward. The packages generally come with cables, spikes, ties, and dowels for additional securing of the logs or timbers. Log houses retain the fully rounded look of logs; some models even retain the bark and rough surface of the felled tree.

The great weight of logs up to a foot in diameter is an important consideration for the do-it-yourselfer. The timbers of timber houses are lighter than logs because they have been milled to flat faces on all four sides. Assembly of timbers is uncomplicated; usually three or four inches thick, they fit together in a tongue-and-groove arrangement that makes the flat faces look more like conventional siding than like logs. This also means that the timber house can achieve a feeling and style more modern than the typically rustic appearance of a log house.

The solid walls of both log and timber houses cut down the amount of trim and finish work required to complete construction. Their strength, solidity, and soundproofing are very appealing qualities; thick wood also functions with fair efficiency as a thermal mass. A mass of wood, moreover, is less vulnerable to fire than a frame of wood members.

Some manufacturers provide bored logs or timbers through which the builder can run plumbing and wiring; when they don't, these utilities have to be carefully planned to run elsewhere. In cold climates, timber houses are sometimes built with double walls, up to nine inches thick, and plumbing and wiring can run through air space between interior and exterior—so can insulation, which does not go into single-wall construction of this type.

In general, less complete (less expensive) packages can be bought from log house manufacturers than from timber house makers. For example, a log house package might include only the logs,

securing devices, and sealants for the walls. More complete packages, especially for timber houses, will include roof assemblies, interior partitions, plumbing and heating systems, and the like.

Buying manufactured housing can be a way to obtain species of wood not generally available in an area. The manufacturers' volume buying allows them to use wood that might not be found at the local lumber yard.

DOMES AND YURTS

Domes and yurts are round or partially round structures that can be built quickly. Domes are the most radical kind of manufactured house; their spherical shape and unconventional interior spaces may be too extreme for some tastes.

Basic mathematics gives a quick idea of the dome's advantages, however. The sphere (a dome house is built from a conventional foundation and floor, so it's not a complete sphere) is the geometric shape which can cover the most floor area with the least surface area. A dome that encloses 1,500 square feet of living area has about 30 percent less surface area than a rectangular house built over the same amount of floor. This means there's 30 percent less material to buy to cover that surface and 30 percent less surface through which heat can escape. For this reason, too, a buyer can have more living (floor) space in a dome than in a conventionally shaped house that costs the same.

The dome, as originally designed by R. Buckminster Fuller, is built up of triangular sections that convey exceptional strength to the whole structure. For its weight, the dome is the strongest structure known. The curved walls give it valuable aerodynamic qualities: outside, winds slip off and around it; inside, air circulates freely and tends to become less stratified than in conventional right-angled rooms.

Because all the structural elements of the dome are contained in the framework of triangles, no load-bearing posts or other walls need to be built. The finished dome is just one open room, however, and some people build partitions to close off bathrooms and bedrooms and to create privacy barriers to sound. Two or more domes can be merged into a larger structure with separate rooms. Vertical partitions can also simplify certain problems created by the curvature, such as building shelves.

Because the dome is a continuous curve, there's no distinction between roof and wall. Usually, a roofing material covers the entire exterior. Triangular windows can be placed in the frame, at the desired height, individually or in clusters. Dormers can be built out from the dome to support rectangular windows, but the framework must not be interrupted in any way to accomplish this or for doors, vents, stovepipes, and the like.

The numerous planes that comprise the surface create some unusual problems in covering the surface inside and out. Rigid materials must be carefully cut to the dimensions of one triangle; while more flexible materials can be worked over larger areas, this must be done without warping or tearing them. The potential for leaks has been a concern in domes, but by now manufacturers have long experience at completely solving the problem.

Assembling the shell of the dome is done easily and very quickly. Covering it can be tedious and strenuous work. Some dome packages deliver complete panels (covered inside and out); some call for piece-by-piece assembly. Plenty of work must be done apart from assembling the contents of the package. Nearly all dome packages provide less than 25 percent (in cost) of a fully finished house.

Contemporary yurts are modifications of the traditional shelter used by Mongolian nomads. Around a circular floor, the structure's walls lean out slightly, and from them the roof rises in a cone. Many of the points made above about the dome's advantages apply to yurts, and its shape eliminates some problems posed by the sphere.

POST-AND-BEAM HOUSES

The post-and-beam framing system is the basis for another class of manufactured housing. As in Bruce Johnson's modified post-and-beam (Chapter Eight), all sorts of designs and styles can be applied over this support system. A ranch-style post-and-beam house may look indistinguishable

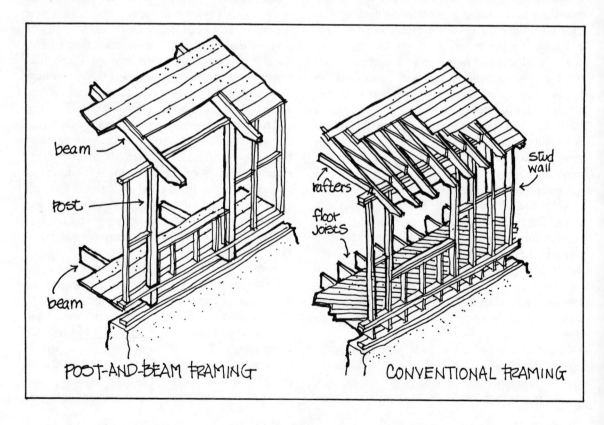

POST-AND-BEAM FRAMING

CONVENTIONAL FRAMING

from a ranch-style house framed with studs, joists, and the rest of a "stick-built" system. But often the virtues of post-and-beam are emphasized and the house will have a different appearance, particularly on the inside.

Posts and beams are much thicker pieces than the two by four members of a stick-built frame. Therefore fewer of them can be placed further apart to hold up the building. These longer spans can accommodate large windows, permit insulation to be installed uninterrupted by studs, and create large open living spaces. It is these large open spaces that give post-and-beam houses their distinctive appearance; often individual posts and beams are left exposed in order to emphasize the house's structural integrity and to let the big timbers be seen.

Many builders believe post-and-beam to be the strongest framing system. It has come down in grand tradition from early New England (and old European) architecture; in the preindustrial era, the timbers were connected by mortise-and-tenon joints and pegs, chiseled and carved by expert craftsmen. Post-and-beam gave way to quicker methods that could be achieved with nails, but it has enjoyed a revival lately because of its strength, flexibility, and traditional associations. (Many of the present-day manufacturers are located in New England.)

A few manufacturers sell packages that are joined in the old-fashioned way, but most post-and-beam frames are now held together by long nails, heavy steel plates, and other such hardware. The packages range from shipments of only a frame assembly to nearly complete houses; the possibility of owner involvement is thus greatly varied, too, from the big job of assembling the former to examples of the latter which manufacturers recommend be put together only by professional builders.

The nature of post-and-beam construction makes add-ons and room expansions relatively easy. Since the load is being borne only on the posts, walls can be opened up without destabilizing the structure. This feature recommends post-and-beam houses to people who are trying to make a start on their house — the "bottom of the line" of several manufacturers may be a sufficient beginning for people with restricted budgets.

PRECUT KITS

All the types of manufactured housing described so far could be labeled "precut" houses. This term also refers to a broad selection of packages that result in a house that's entirely conventional in framing and appearance. Precut house packages are truly kits. They contain all, or nearly all, the pieces of a house, which the buyer assembles. These packages are therefore of great interest to owner-builders; construction, following complete directions provided by the manufacturer, is not difficult or especially strenuous. Dealing with all the pieces does take lots of time and patience, though.

Unfortunately, an important consideration in any building project is theft and vandalism. Many house packages take weeks or months to complete and thus will be on the site for a long time after delivery, creating a real security problem. Planning the project must include ways to enclose and lock up building materials. Some packages are designed so that a basic shell goes up quickly and materials for the rest of the house can be secured inside it. Another strategy is to buy an incomplete package and purchase additional materials locally as they're needed. But to some extent this approach defeats the purpose of manufactured housing — namely, that the package includes everything that is needed, already measured and cut. Building a shed or detached garage first, or installing a temporary structure, are other ways of dealing with the problem.

Figuring for theft is a significant contributor to the high cost of conventional housing, since many contractors routinely order 10 percent more lumber, plywood, concrete, wire, and so forth than is actually called for in the plans. Houses which are assembled rapidly avoid this problem and, of course, can be moved into much sooner than the time-consuming types. Panelized, modular, and sectional houses are the categories that meet this description. Most of the assembly of these is done at a factory, and only a few large pieces are shipped to the site. "Panelized" usually refers to preassembled wall sections — a finished sandwich inside and out, including insulation, plumbing, wiring, and windows. Some manufacturers ship a wall panel that is open on the interior so that plumbing and wiring can be installed and inspected on-site. This type also leaves room for the do-it-yourselfer to get involved in finish work. Panelized floor and roof sections are available too.

Some open-wall types come in sizes that can be maneuvered and joined by amateur crews. Others, and the closed-wall types, are long and heavy — as much as eight by forty feet — and require cranes and professionals.

Industrial processes enable wall panels to be manufactured more exactly than conventional walls can be built at a building site. Specialized fastening and sealing methods can greatly reduce infiltration.

Another industrial contribution is the completely prefinished mechanical or utility core. Whole bathrooms, kitchens, heating/cooling systems, and plumbing systems can be made in factories, shipped to the building site, and lifted into place in the house by a crane or boom truck. These cores are available from some panelized house manufacturers.

Again the advantage here is speed. Being able to move in rapidly is a key feature for some buyers. Some cost saving occurs since construction time is radically reduced and building loans can be for shorter terms. The need for expensive labor for on-site finish work is reduced when the panel is finished at the factory. But the more work that is performed by others, the closer the final cost approaches the cost of conventional construction.

Modular and sectional houses carry manufactured housing to the present limits of prefabrication. Work on these types is done almost entirely at the factory, and the owner's involvement amounts to telling the dealer what to include in the factory product. Interior decoration is often all that is left for the owner to do.

Modular and sectional houses typically arrive at the site in two pieces — lengthwise halves — which are lifted onto a waiting foundation and connected. Usually these are one-story structures, but two-story houses are possible using the same techniques.

Conventional building techniques are used, but factory processes for combining them differ from on-site techniques. Glue-bonding floor and wall sections, for example, is a process that can only be carried out in a factory setting.

Because such large modules must be transported, manufacturers of modular and sectional houses generally distribute them to dealers and customers in their home and adjacent states. But it's a big industry and there's a choice of manufacturers in each section of the country.

MOBILE HOMES

Mobile homes are yet another category of manufactured housing. They're closest in concept to modular and sectional houses, but there are important distinctions to be made. A touchy issue here is the tarnished reputation of mobile homes, a reputation that the manufactured housing industry wants to change.

The historical background of the contemporary mobile home lies in the development of trailers which, hitched to cars or trucks, were truly mobile homes. These first began to appear in the 1930s, but to meet housing shortages after World War II, many were unhitched and permanently occupied in trailer parks. Early trailers looked very little like conventional houses and seemed transient even in trailer parks. The idea that they could be satisfactory housing was widely viewed with scorn and dismissed. Mobile homes were taxed as vehicles, not as real property. Many early models were, in fact, shoddily built.

Long-term damage had been done to their reputation, but mobile homes continued to evolve in the direction of permanent housing while recreational vehicles appeared to meet the demand for traveling shelter. Today most mobile homes are about as mobile as modular and sectional houses — that is, they travel from factory to site over public highways.

Modular and sectional houses, however, do rest on conventional foundations and in every way match the appearance of conventional housing. Mobile homes are built on a steel chassis that rests on a simple configuration of concrete blocks, not a true foundation. And their shape and appearance tend to be characteristically unique and unlike the conventional house.

Manufactured houses and mobile homes are built to conform to somewhat different sets of state and federal standards. Where each can be placed in a community has been a matter of difference also; manufactured houses generally can go wherever conventional houses can, but mobile homes are in many communities restricted to mobile home parks or zones where all units must be mobiles.

This discrimination appears to be gradually ending, though. In 1981, California put a new law into effect which allows mobile homes to be placed wherever single-family houses are allowed, as long as their rooflines and exteriors conform to the look of conventional housing. Conventional appearance is becoming increasingly typical as mobile home manufacturers, spurred by the economic pressures on the housing market, bid for a greater percentage of that market by making more widely acceptable products. With skirts around their edges, with patios, decks, and landscaping, and with more options in roofs and siding, mobile homes are managing to look more and more the way the general public thinks houses should look.

DOING IT YOURSELF

Clearly, performing most of the work of building your house yourself is the most direct way to lower the total cash outlay for the project. Equally clearly, there are personal costs paid in lieu of the cash to someone else: building is a grand undertaking and a demanding experience. It shouldn't be undertaken lightly but can be immensely rewarding — also boring, exhausting, creative, and memorable. As dozens of books and magazine articles will caution you, building a house is an enormous undertaking for the amateur — *always* more work and time than it had been projected to take.

Many of the readers of this book, even without prior experience, could successfully build the Cotati winning designs. The solarium house and the gangnail house call for prefabricated elements which, once on the site, are easy to work with. The double envelope house is an unusual design but not much more complicated to build than a single-wall stud frame. Every house involves standard plumbing and wiring, foundation, siding, roofing, and finish work.

The contest was not held with owner-builders in mind, since it was intended to have mass applicability and most people in fact buy their homes already built. Still, many owner-builders buy plans for their house rather than design it themselves from scratch (and plans for the Cotati winners are all available from the designers, whose addresses are listed at the end of the book).

FINANCING

The task of financing your affordable house is the inevitable "bottom line" of the entire undertaking. All of your interest in the type of house envisioned here will come to nothing if you can't pay for it. To a large degree, the only financial advice that emerges from the Cotati contest is the obvious: pay less.

Assuming that you will have to borrow money in order to own your home, having to borrow less of it is the most direct way of keeping monthly payments on the loan manageable. At 15 percent interest, the monthly payment necessary to amortize a $30,000 thirty-year loan is $379.20. Monthly payment on a $20,000 loan for the same term and interest is $252.80.

Dealing with an officer of a bank or savings and loan to obtain financing for a small house will mean convincing the banker not only that you are a reasonable risk but also that the house is. The well-known conservatism of bankers stems from the gloomy possibilities that can lead to the bank owning the house (foreclosure); more than any other institution, banks want houses to conform to current standards and to be as luxurious and convenient as possible so that they will have the theoretically optimum chances for being easily resold. Houses that are too different from the norm look especially suspicious to bankers; hence the concern of so many designers, builders, and city officials for conventionality and mass appeal.

Many lenders currently balk at making a loan on a house with no central heating system. In their eyes, the combination of passive-solar and wood heat is insufficient. The Cotati-type houses thus have to prove themselves before they can be built — a "catch 22" and a vicious circle that reinforces the crisis in housing. The Cotati contest, by publicizing this type of house, begins the ⟨ ⟩ of changing minds and attitudes. There ⟨ ⟩ bankers — and their number is growin⟨ ⟩ lend money for houses of this type.

103

High interest rates and deep recession in the housing industry create a situation in which the professionals involved in a housing transaction must be, above all, flexible. While what is called "creative financing" is regarded as chaos by many, a borrower who grasps the fact that there are numerous options is in position to find an advantageous one.

TAX CONSIDERATIONS

Tax laws present the individual with certain advantages that slightly ease the burden of financing. Interest payments on loans are deductible items in figuring income taxes. Since most of each monthly payment during the first years of a loan goes to paying interest, this is a large chunk that can be partially recovered in tax savings. Property taxes (and other local and state taxes) are deductible items too in figuring federal income tax.

Deductible items lower a person's total taxable income. This total in turn is taxed according to which tax bracket it falls in. While deductible items will not help certain taxpayers with modest incomes, tax credits are subtracted directly from anyone's tax bill. Tax credits are allowed for expenditures on energy-conserving materials (such as insulation) and on solar equipment; many states and the federal government instituted these credits to reward energy conservation and solar installation.

Many of the laws which instituted these credits, however, will remain in effect for only a few years, an incentive to take advantage of them soon. The Internal Revenue Service and state taxing agencies issue regulations and decisions regarding the specific use of these tax credits. One IRS ruling said that credit could be claimed only for solar equipment that was installed for the single purpose of using solar energy — a flat-plate collector, for example. This ruling has gloomy implications for passive solar, since the point of good passive-solar design is to integrate solar energy collection and storage into the actual walls, floors, windows, and the rest of the house — a multiple rather than a single use.

In the hard number analysis that must precede any building project, active solar may come out ahead of passive if it significantly pays for itself through tax credits and passive doesn't. But tax laws and interpretations of them change constantly; be sure to obtain current information if you're considering such an analysis.

COOPERATIVES

Rather than going it alone and trying to resolve the problem of affordable housing wholly as an individual, you may find more opportunities by working with others in some form of cooperative organization. Housing co-ops have been established to buy and manage existing apartment buildings, to finance, build, and occupy developments of single-family houses, and to deal with nearly every other housing situation. Co-ops are not by definition organizations for people with modest income; some high-rent apartment buildings in Manhattan, for example, are set up as co-ops.

As an organization, a co-op is in line for foundation grants, government funding, and bank loans that individuals have no chance of obtaining. In particular, an organization rather than an individual is likely to qualify for the subsidies and low-interest loans that are available to people with low incomes. The very existence of the co-op, especially if it has a good reputation, is strong evidence to the lender of a good risk.

A condominium is another type of group housing organization, but here the individual condo member is typically someone who could afford to buy a primary residence independently. The condominium leaves power in the individual's hands; the co-op puts decision-making power in the hands of the group. Neither is an absolute arrangement; as with the Manhattan co-ops, the condominium is not necessarily exclusive housing.

In a condominium arrangement, each unit of housing is separately owned. In a cooperative, the co-op owns all the units while the occupants own shares of the co-op itself. In either form, the grounds around the buildings and whatever group facilities exist — party room, laundry, swimming pool — belong to an association of all members.

By means of its bylaws and various restrictions on the deed to its property, a co-op can ensure that its housing units remain affordable for years after construction. Such a deed restriction might, for example, limit the amount of equity each member has in the property so that when a member sells shares of the co-op, they have not appreciated beyond a certain low limit. This arrangement protects the property from speculation and the effects of inflation of surrounding property values. (Real estate transfer costs are eliminated because the original deed remains in effect.) It also means that a new member can gain access to the co-op at proportionally the same level of income as a departing member. Departing members do make a small return on their initial investment, but they forego the big profits that house selling often brings.

For people who couldn't own a house otherwise, this loss of big profits is not too great a sacrifice to make. Obviously, by its very name, a co-op insists that people work together, a process that can be arduous and frustrating. But the co-op method, which has been around — successfully — for a long time, is an important option for people who are determined to obtain housing that's their own.

Another version of the co-op approach is called "sweat equity" — an arrangement by which each member of a group helps to build all the houses the group will eventually occupy, usually in an ongoing co-op organization. This arrangement is particularly well suited for use in rural areas, especially since much of the funding for it comes from the Farmers Home Administration of the federal government.

As the trend toward smaller housing units strengthens, both co-ops and condominiums will become increasingly popular as ways for people to obtain more housing than they could afford on their own. Without such social forms that enable people to get along better together (outside of government auspices), some individuals can be isolated and ultimately weakened by exclusive reliance upon themselves.

Chapter Eleven
The House in Your Future

There can be no true conclusion to this book. The real conclusion, if there is to be one, lies with you, as you make choices, learn more, and perhaps build your house. Certainly the houses described here constitute a major shift in direction for Americans. The ideas in them and behind them respond not only to present-day economic realities but also to a long-term vision that is only now coming into meaningful focus. This is a vision of how we can go on living for *generations,* a sense and understanding of sustainability.

SUSTAINABILITY: TAKING THE LONG VIEW

There is some evidence to indicate that we are merely in a time of transition — painful, yes, but transitory — on the way to a bigger, better future than anything attained before now. For example, we are told that there is plenty of energy locked up in sources we're now beginning to tap; because it's not yet "on line," there must be a transition, and it is uncomfortable.

Furthermore, goes this reasoning, renewed strong growth in the American economy will again spread the constantly increasing benefits of our system to more and more of our people. Technology has raised our living standards repeatedly and dramatically in the past; it will continue to do so. In other words, we do not need to make major changes in our routines, ideas, values, standards, goals — only keep doing what we have done so well in the past.

We are talking about the future, so we can hardly view it with certainty. Nonetheless, the concept of sustainability strikes me as being ultimately a stronger bet than relying on the pattern of the past to propel us into the future. By sustainability I mean the measurement and evaluation of a process or product according to whether it can be repeated or reproduced indefinitely with *all* costs taken into account.

In the case of housing — the process and the product — I obviously mean houses such as the ones the contest at Cotati produced as winners. But clearly the variations — of size, design, convenience — are myriad; the houses described here aren't winners in any exclusive way, only as good models of The Sustainable House. Designed in the eighties to last far into the twenty-first century, they recognize the long-term costs of using land, building materials, and energy, and they consider the sheer cost of living to be paid by all of us throughout the period.

Using sustainability as a criterion for decision making in many fields forces us to study the future *and* to know the past. The point is not that we're running out of things but that we have to keep making sure that we don't. Resources must be protected, repaired, nourished — sustained — even as they are being used.

A good example is reforestation. As a prime renewable resource, the nation's forests would benefit from many years of steady employment of people planting trees, repairing damage to timberland, clearing streams, thinning overgrown acreage, removing brush and trees that compete with commercially valuable species, maintaining thousands of miles of existing logging roads, cutting firewood, and much more. This work needs doing. The goal of sustained-yield logging, an already widely acknowledged example of sustainability, requires this sort of forest management in order to be realized.

Another example is the national network of highways, in particular the interstate system. Finished for the most part in the seventies, its crumbling and decay will be a major problem of the eighties and beyond. This brilliant expression of our national love for the automobile has become a "resource," too, and one that must be continuously repaired if it is to be sustained. Early reports indicate that shortfalls in funding for repairs threaten, on balance, to lower the quality of these roads upon which so much transportation of freight and passengers depends.

Part of the sustainability that the Cotati-type houses imply would be a steadily employed force in the construction trades and a freeing of the construction industry from its cyclical instability. Acting on a strong commitment to build smaller houses, the industry would find itself in a larger market of people who also need housing, many of whom could get it if the amount they need to borrow were substantially less — even at high interest rates.

The smart designs for the small house of the eighties and nineties will be built quickly and simply; there's no other way for them to be affordable. Building more houses per year for less profit on each — a volume approach — isn't in theory a losing proposition. Small houses may be a more reliable, stable, sustainable basis for that industry than larger, more luxurious houses whose construction is an erratic and unpredictable business.

YOU AND YOUR HOUSE

This sort of enthusiasm sounds good, but the daily practice of business and industry and government is not this way. The smaller picture, the shorter term, and the immediate gain are the typical foci of attention. It's someone else's job to deal with side effects that will show up years later.

Earlier I said that "the houses described here constitute a major shift in direction for Americans." Building them is easy enough; but is there a will to build them, a long enough vision to see the wisdom in them?

You respond to these houses and these ideas out of your own experience and view of the world. This, too, is why I say that the conclusion of this book lies ultimately with you, the individual. It is you who has to decide where and how to live during the years ahead. As an individual you do not, in fact, have much power to influence the kinds of houses that will be built in this country in the years ahead. Nevertheless, your understanding of this type of house, and your support, can contribute to a climate of opinion in which change does take place.

Whether through economic constraints felt in the present or through conscious vision of a likely long-term future, people will see the need for this house. Those who see that need can express their demand directly to contractors, bankers, architects, building and planning officials, investors, educators, opinion makers, and politicians.

In the mid-1970s there were so few solar houses of any kind in the United States that reports on solar technology had to refer to a literal handful of individual homes rather than to types of designs. The transition to solar has just begun. If the economic power to insist on these houses being built in great numbers requires a constituency, that constituency has only begun to form.

No matter where you live, there are twenty-four hours in your day and you spend most of them busy or asleep, with momentary seasonings of humor, boredom, happiness, and glumness mixed in. You like to be with people *and* you like to be alone. You like to go out *and* you like to stay home. There are a few things that are really special to you and you enjoy them when time, money, and other obligations allow.

What has this got to do with housing? Well, houses are for living in, and how you live is going to influence the sort of house you want. If you're roughly the person I've been sketching, I think you'll be well served by a small, efficient, *smart* house. You'll fill it with things you use and like; the things that there's no room for, and the things your house will never be, are simply on the other side of boundaries you've already recognized. You are not fighting it; in fact, most of the time you feel good about traveling light.

If you're giving serious consideration to owning a house like the ones described here, then we can hazard some more guesses about you. Because you want to own your home, you are prepared to work at it, if not on the building, then on maintenance and improvement. Knowing that your house will be at the lower end of the price range of new houses, we can figure that your income is modest too — and that you're not counting on it to skyrocket any time soon. Nevertheless, you are steady, responsible, and secure enough — in your thoughts as well as in your budget — to commit yourself to the obligations of long-term financing. You have *some* ability to pay. Sound like anyone you know?

TAKING THE FIRST STEPS

Here are some unglamorous but down-to-earth and useful ideas for taking more steps toward the goals and dreams you have about your home.

Enroll in a class at the community college or adult education center in your area. Get your hands on some of the materials that a house is made of by studying woodworking, electricity, solar energy, and the like.

Analyze the house or apartment you're living in now. Check out the elements of its heating and cooling systems; find out how they work. Measure your rooms and draw a floor plan. Notice how much space is used for circulation and for storage. Judge for yourself how much is enough, how much is being wasted by poor design, and how much is simply unnecessary for the way you live.

Look at your utility bill and try to find less costly solutions to the problem of staying warm in winter. Cursing utility companies, government commissions, and OPEC countries isn't nearly as productive as doing something for yourself. Install a woodburning stove or fireplace insert and get used to the routines of obtaining and handling firewood. Buy and install weatherstripping and insulation, including movable insulation for windows.

Study your place for possible solar retrofitting. Even if you don't intend to actually add anything, just analyzing the solar potentials and problems is a good way to move further into the working details of attached greenhouses, breadbox water heaters, flat-plate collectors, and the rest. Pay attention to solar orientation and the seasonal differences caused by trees, overhangs, neighboring structures, and the weather.

Make sketches, drawings, and diagrams as a tool for clarifying principles and solving problems. If the cost is reasonable, add or remodel a room with the deliberate aim of gaining construction experience. Find a carpenter who will work with you, directing the work but letting you learn firsthand about as many aspects of it as you're willing to encounter.

"Learning by doing" has become a commonplace of thinking about education, so familiar that we may forget the enormous wisdom of it. For your house to emerge — to stand on the ground as a real built thing — requires that you have a steadily strengthening grasp of concepts, facts, skills, and materials. You've got a lot to learn, and the ways you learn best matter. Not the abstractions of school studies or the passive pleasures of reading about things far out of your life, this kind of learning has a deliberate goal. There are many ways to reach it, but you need to become conscious of the ways that are smoothest for you. What don't you already know? What worries or scares you about accomplishing your goals?

Don't take these remarks as a devaluation of reading. Use the library! There are so many books on the related topics of construction, design, home technology, home economics, etc., etc., that any library will have at least a starting point for further research and study. Look at lots of books until you develop a feeling for which ones are really communicating to you, which ones are too hard, too easy, too fancy, too out-of-date. Practice reading floor plans, wall and roof details, elevations, and other construction diagrams so that they become a more familiar language to you.

Use the local newspaper to gain an understanding of the current climate of real estate, building, and land use in your area. Look at some model homes. Is there a solar promotion group? Such associations often sponsor home tours, workshops, and lectures. Attend city council and planning commission meetings to watch the government process in action. Ask in the right department to look at zoning maps, general plans, and building codes.

Gaze as far into the future as you can and predict the various housing costs you'll be facing — in three, five, fifteen, forty years. Do you think your income will keep you covered then? Or do you need to start making changes now?

Weigh the importance of housing issues in your life. Our other responsibilities, hobbies, and enthusiasms all compete for attention, and it's difficult to set any aside. But if the concerns of this book truly matter to you, then make room in your mind, your schedule, and your budget for dealing with them. It is simple enough to go through life just taking what's commonly available; but if you make it your goal, you can seek out and ultimately have the uncommon — and sustainable — house.

Appendix

What Happened in Cotati

Cotati, California, showed early evidence of a penchant for original planning ideas. Its first town plan, dating from the 1890s, was one of only two in the United States to spread out in a hexagon. The six-sided town plaza was designed by Newton Smyth for founder Thomas Page, and each of the surrounding streets was named after one of Page's sons. The name Cotati is derived from Kotate, a local Indian.

The city has for some years also had a reputation as a politically liberal and active place. During a recent period that activity was above all rancorous, with loud noises rising out of several issues at once. In a small headline above a report on one of these, the *Rohnert Park—Cotati Clarion* asked pointedly: "A Cotati meeting minus conflict?"

It's quite a small city, population 3,570, which finds itself swept by a very big wave of growth. Located about sixty miles north of San Francisco, Cotati is at the northern periphery of the Bay Area, a geographic region that may have a specific definition somewhere but whose boundaries seem to expand.

Petaluma, the larger (population 34,500) city nine miles south of Cotati, became well known several years ago when it passed a growth-limitation ordinance in response to the same wave of growth. Bus service makes it possible to commute to work in downtown San Francisco from either place.

At the same time the city of Santa Rosa (population 84,700), nine miles north of Cotati, is becoming a major center in its own right, attracting new businesses and industry that put additional development pressure on the communities surrounding it, including Cotati.

Between Cotati and Santa Rosa is Rohnert Park (population 22,695), a city built literally from scratch during the past fifteen years along with the steady development of Sonoma State University. So Cotati is something of a college town, too; its downtown area, close to the university campus, has a collection of restaurants and shops to serve a college crowd.

All these communities are in Sonoma County, a beautiful part of Northern California well known for its vineyards and wineries. While these agricultural land uses dominate the county north of Santa Rosa, urban uses have steadily reversed the formerly rural air of the southern half. Petaluma, once a major egg-producing center, is now mostly residential subdivisions.

To get an idea of the problems of growth in the area, consider that Hewlett-Packard Corporation, a giant electronics firm, is at the time this is written attempting to site a new plant in Rohnert Park that would employ approximately six thousand workers.

Quite obviously, phenomenal growth such as this has enormous impact on housing in Cotati. Land inside the city limits sells for an estimated $150,000 per acre. But very few small parcels are for sale, even at such a price; most undeveloped land is held by developers.

Credit for the idea of the Affordable Housing Competition belongs to Eve O'Rourke, a spirited and insistent member of the Cotati city council. At the time she proposed the contest, O'Rourke was mayor, a revolving position; before she was elected to the council, she had served on the local planning commission. Out of her years of dealing with all the city's business, she had gained close knowledge of — and tremendous frustration with — the particular problem of affordable housing.

Perhaps more than many other communities, Cotati has a high percentage of small households, especially students and other members of the university. These tend to be people with modest incomes, too. O'Rourke says she got tired of waiting for developers to build housing for these households. She says, "They're still building bigger, more ornate houses all the time, and the cost is not coming down. I had to come up with a way to force the cost of housing down."

The result of her conviction was the contest idea; a one-page announcement and explanation was issued in December 1980. The only opposition to the affordable housing project was voiced by some realtors, O'Rourke says, who "never missed a chance to say that it would create 'more slums' in Cotati. They just couldn't grasp the idea of low-*cost* housing. I guess they automatically equate it with low-*income* housing, even though low-income people don't own houses. We had to come up with everything and just figure it out for ourselves. We were initiating a new concept."

The judging did take place in orderly fashion in the spring of 1981. The three members of the design review committee (a permanent city body) used several criteria and awarded points to each design according to how well each criterion was met. The criteria were: (1) energy-efficient design, both site and structure; (2) cost-effectiveness of materials and methods of construction; (3) aesthetics; (4) practicality for future application; (5) quality of application and ability of designer to carry through; (6) cost-effectiveness of financing and the building process; and (7) adaptability to different household sizes and types. A design could be awarded 1 to 16 points for each of the first five criteria and 1 to 10 points for the latter two, for a possible total of 100 points.

Judging on this basis produced eleven semifinalists. These were then reevaluated and given a single number of points (to a maximum of 10) by each judge. Averaging the three judges' awards produced the final ranking.

With the six winners selected, there was an encouraging flood of positive publicity and inquiries from individuals and other cities wanting to know how it had been done. But it hadn't been done.

The hardest part — making the designs a reality as housing — remained.

According to O'Rourke, if the only actions needed had been ones the city could do itself, then "we could have rammed it through" without much delay or complication. "But we had to deal with banks and with the state."

Extraordinarily high interest rates for production and purchase loans were being charged by lenders throughout this period, a direct result of monetary policy set by the federal government. As has been noted, housing feels this economic pinch especially severely, so Cotati was faced with trying to operate in an atmosphere of discouragement and glum waiting for conditions to improve.

These conditions, of course, had helped stimulate the contest in the first place, but now city officials had to confront them head on. Despite the favorable publicity, the typical lender responded with some skepticism about the houses' unconventional design and resale potential. Some bankers wanted the houses to be built with conventional heating systems — in effect suggesting that passive-solar heating and woodstoves could only be regarded as secondary contributors to heating. Others wanted to know more about the ownership plans than had been worked out. Banks naturally would not want to create a mortgage that would be assumed by someone who couldn't make the payments. Given the confusion between low-cost and low-income housing, and the fact that the city had not worked out the ownership plan, the lenders' hesitation was at least understandable. (In keeping with the goals of the contest, it had already been decided that the deeds to the houses would contain clauses permanently restricting the allowable jump in later resale prices — to *keep* the houses affordable.)

"The city" during this time came to be staff personnel rather than city council or design review committee members. While city manager Rory Robinson, administrative assistant Richard Ward, and general services director Richard Box were all supportive of the project, each found that he had inherited an unexpectedly large and knotty load of work to do in expediting construction of the winning designs.

As a small staff in an era of tight budgets, these people were already hard pressed to keep up with the normal flow of city business. Then, as if to complicate matters further, conflict over other issues generated a recall campaign against two city council members and city manager Robinson suddenly resigned. This uproar contributed to an air of tension and uncertainty that tended to push the contest into the background.

Nevertheless, the city did take such actions as it could on its own, including the public hearing process and final approval of a zoning change to allow cluster-type housing (PUDs). Cotati already had an ordinance making PUDs a zoning option, so this step was uncomplicated. Similarly, surveying, soils testing, and preliminary planning for city services to the site went ahead without much difficulty.

Following the judging, several of the winning designers held a series of meetings with the design review committee at which, among other things, they agreed upon a site plan. The plan, largely the work of house designer Bruce Johnson, laid out a mix of one, two, and three-bedroom units in four clusters on the 1.8-acre site. A total of nineteen units would include the winning designs plus duplicates and expanded versions of several of them. Clustering allows individual units to be oriented for optimal solar exposure and draws adjacent units into a small community.

A service area of driveway, parking spaces, and trash enclosures is concentrated for all residents in a strip along the western edge of the property and incorporates the four large existing trees, thus keeping the units away from the shade. A walkway, terminating in a "social deck," ties each cluster to the service area. The walkways, plus a 7,000-square-foot recreation area and some smaller common areas, are held jointly and maintained by the homeowners association. Each dwelling unit has its own lot, which encloses the unit, a patio, and a sizable private area. With this pattern, costs associated with the common area are to be minimized. Both the parking areas and the social decks include storage facilities.

The plan calls for a ground cover of lawn in the large common areas and for native plants and flowers that don't require watering in the remainder. One of its goals, too, was to present adjacent properties with "attractive and appropriate" views.

While the site plan manages to organize and unify structures, services, and landscaping on the property, several people involved in designing it wondered aloud how harmoniously the different designs would blend when built together. This lack of a unified architectural style would presumably recall the experimental nature of the contest but might look odd or disjointed once the contest was history.

One specific matter the city had to address in making its zoning changes dealt with parking spaces. The local ordinance under which the site would be zoned a PUD calls for two covered parking spaces per unit. But the site plan proposed fewer spaces than this requirement. In supporting this change, the staff report noted:

> The unique nature of this totally price-controlled project is such that it is expected that residents will own and use less than two cars [per unit]. Therefore, in order to provide an attractive site, as free of asphalt as possible, it is proposed to ask for two variances: one to provide 34 spaces, 85 percent of the ordinance requirement of 40, and just the number that would be required if there were apartments (7 three-bedrooms at 2 spaces/unit = 14, plus 13 one- and two-bedrooms at 1.5 spaces/unit = 19.5; 19.5 + 14 = 33.5). It is believed that the multiple family standard is sufficient, and though 40 spaces can easily be accommodated on the site (one of the first site plans had 40), such a design has a negative effect on overall appearance with no apparent positive result.
>
> Further, covering all the spaces would present a massive, monolithic appearance detrimental to the open, airy appearance of the site; there is no demonstrable need for two covered spaces for this type of housing unit.

The variance was approved. After the site plan had been developed and approved, the meetings among city officials and contest winners addressed the major problems surrounding financing and construction — and fell, unfortunately, into sharp disagreement.

An original condition of the contest, not stated in its announcement but understood by the finalists, was that each entrant should have the ability to arrange personally for financing one unit. Having heard resistance from institutional lenders, the city decided to insist upon these arrangements in order to get the first cluster built. It appeared that four of the winners would also be able to finance a

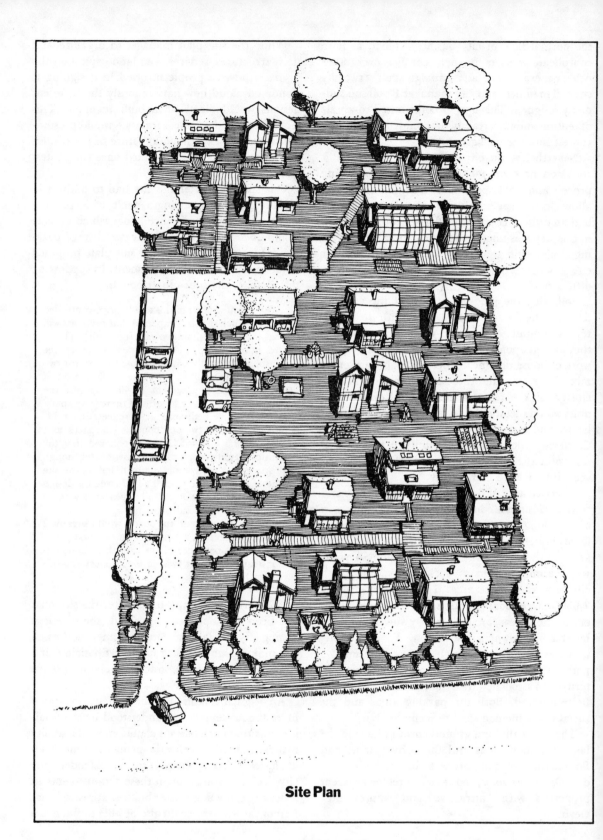

Site Plan

second unit each; these four would also be built, in a second phase of construction, for a total of ten units. Once the ten units were complete, a local savings and loan association had promised to offer mortgage money to buyers. It was also assumed that with this much accomplished, other lenders would come forward with loans for the final nine units.

The problems with this plan were not with the financing but with the obligations and responsibilities legally attached to the roles the winners would have to play in it. For instance, each designer would have to act as a building contractor and thereby incur the need for licensing, bonding, and insurance such as worker's compensation.

Two of the winners are already contractors and fully familiar with these requirements; but for the rest these were new, expensive, and unwanted burdens. Profit margins were already projected as very slim; in fact the main benefit was likely to come in the form of publicity for their work. Depending upon specific budgets, it appeared that some of the winners might actually lose money by putting up their design for less than $20,000.

This book was completed before these issues and details could be resolved and cannot report on the final outcome. Regardless of the outcome, the designs stimulated by Cotati's call for affordable housing have already proved valuable in raising questions and bringing forth alternatives.

The Design Contest

THE CONTEST ANNOUNCEMENT

Can the $20,000 House Be Built?

The City Council of the City of Cotati wishes to open a contest to encourage the development of housing designs which offer alternatives to conventional housing types, and will award building space and water and electrical hookups for five different alternative-type housing units. The winners of the contest will have the opportunity to build their models in a cluster suitable for demonstration, and exhibit them for one year. The city will publicize the models and actively encourage further housing development of this type — affordable housing units. At the end of the one year period the buildings may be sold to individuals, moved, acquired by the city, or recycled in some way by the builder.

It is the intent of the city to attract developers who will build affordable housing in Cotati; the contest will draw attention to the need for a change in the type and price of housing which is currently being provided by the building industry. The contest will be judged by the Design Review Committee.

Judging Criteria

The cost of the housing unit shall not exceed $20,000. That figure must include building inspection and city permit fees, although in this contest these fees will be waived.

Housing designs will: (1) conform to local building codes; (2) decrease as many amenities as possible, for example, garage, appliances, extra bathroom, carpeting, paved driveway and walkway, and so on; (3) make use of a passive heating and cooling system; (4) make use of recycled building materials where feasible.

We are looking for the best house at the lowest cost. Creative interpretation of building codes may be necessary, and recommendations by the building designer for possible code changes are welcome.

An individual unit design may be submitted which is intended to be part of a cluster, or have common walls with another unit, or be stacked with another unit. In such cases a site plan shall be submitted to indicate the unit's placement.

THE WINNING HOUSE DESIGNERS

The Northbay House
Northbay Architects, Post Office Box 358,
  Santa Rosa, California 95402

The VPS House
VPS Associates, Post Office Box 582,
  Albion, California 95410

The Open Plan House
Bonnie Pencek, 11303 Skyline Road,
  Forestville, California 95436
Diana Samhradh, Post Office Box 481,
  Occidental, California 95465
Georgia Stubbs, 2236 Schaeffer Road,
  Sebastopol, California 95472

The Double Envelope House
Randolph Greenwald, Post Office Box 1187,
  Ukiah, California 95482

The Solarium House
John Roberts and Don Moser,
  6815 South Santa Rosa Avenue, Suite A,
  Cotati, California 94928

The Gangnail House
Bruce Johnson, 2628 15th Avenue,
  San Francisco, California 94127

Bibliography

In addition to the following publications, a series of pamphlets for homeowners has been published by the Small Homes Council—Building Research Council, Champaign-Urbana, University of Illinois.

American Building. James Marston Fitch. Cambridge, Massachusetts: Houghton Mifflin Co., 1972.

Architecture and Energy: Conserving Energy Through Rational Design. Richard G. Stein. Garden City, New York: Anchor Press/Doubleday, 1978.

At Home in the Sun: An Open-House Tour of Solar Homes in the United States. Norah Deakin Davis and Linda Lindsey. Charlotte, Vermont: Garden Way Publishing, 1979.

Build Your Own Solar Water Heater. Stu Campbell. Charlotte, Vermont: Garden Way Publishing, 1978.

Building a Sustainable Society. Lester R. Brown. New York: W. W. Norton & Co., 1981.

California Affordable Housing Competition. Final report. Robert Schaeffer. Sacramento, California: Governor's Office of Appropriate Technology, 1982.

The Complete Book of Prefabs, Kits, and Manufactured Houses. Prepared by the editors of *Consumer Guide.* New York: Fawcett Columbine, 1981.

Design with Climate: Bioclimatic Approach to Architectural Regionalism. Victor Olygay. Princeton, New Jersey: Princeton University Press, 1963.

Direct Use of the Sun's Energy. Farrington Daniels. New York: Ballantine Books, 1964.

Handmade Hot Water Systems. Art Sussman and Richard Frazier. Point Arena, California: Garcia River Press, 1978.

The Last Landscape. William H. Whyte. Garden City, New York: Doubleday, 1968.

Low-Cost, Energy-Efficient Shelter for the Owner Builder. Edited by Eugene Eccli. Emmaus, Pennsylvania: Rodale Press, 1975.

New Energy Technologies for Buildings. Richard Schoen, Alan S. Hirshberg, and Jerome M. Weingart. Cambridge, Massachusetts: Ballinger Publishing Co., 1975.

The Next Whole Earth Catalog. Prepared by the staff of *The Co-Evolution Quarterly.* San Francisco, California: Point/Random House, 1980.

Other Homes and Garbage: Designs for Self-Sufficient Living. Jim Leckie, Gil Masters, Harry Whitehouse, and Lily Young. San Francisco, California: Sierra Club Books, 1975.

The Owner-Builder and the Code. Ken Kern, Rob Thallon, and Ted Kogon. North Fork, California: Owner-Builder Publications, 1976.

Passive Solar Energy: The Homeowner's Guide to Natural Heating and Cooling. Bruce Anderson and Malcolm Wells. Andover, Massachusetts: Brick House Publishing Co., 1981.

The Passive Solar Energy Book: A Complete Guide to Passive Solar Home, Greenhouse, and Building Design. Edward Mazria. Emmaus, Pennsylvania: Rodale Press, 1975.

A Pattern Language: Towns, Buildings, Construction. Christopher Alexander, Sara Ishikawa, and Murray Silverstein. New York: Oxford University Press, 1977.

People Power: What Communities Are Doing to Counter Inflation. Washington, D.C.: U.S. Office of Consumer Affairs, 1980.

Present Value: Constructing a Sustainable Future. Sacramento, California: Governor's Office of Appropriate Technology, Office of Planning and Research, 1979.

Site Planning. Kevin Lynch. Cambridge, Massachusetts: MIT Press, 1962.

Solar Control and Shading Devices. Aladar Olygay and Victor Olygay. Princeton, New Jersey: Princeton University Press, 1957.

Solar for Your Present Home: San Francisco Bay Area Edition. Berkeley Solar Group. Sacramento, California: Energy Commission, 1977.

Solar Gain: Winners of the Passive Solar Design Competition. Sacramento, California: Energy Commission, Governor's Office of Appropriate Technology, 1980.

The Toilet Paper. Sim Van der Ryn. Santa Barbara, California: Capra Press, 1978.

Village Homes: Solar House Designs. David Bainbridge, Judy Corbett, and John Hofacre. Emmaus, Pennsylvania: Rodale Press, 1979.

Wood Heat. John Vivian. Emmaus, Pennsylvania: Rodale Press, 1978.

Wood Heat Safety. Jay W. Shelton. Charlotte, Vermont: Garden Way Publishing Co., 1979.

Your Engineered House. Rex Roberts. New York: M. Evans & Co., 1964.

Index

A

Active-solar systems, 13; heating water, 74; mechanical devices, 13

Affordable Housing Competition, 9, 113, 118; criteria, 114, 118; financing a condition, 115; judging, 114

Air lock, 49

Antifreeze systems: flat-plate collectors, 44

Assembler, 78

Automatic controllers: flat-plate collectors, 44; timers, 93

B

Backup heating and hot water systems, 93; Cotati houses, 13; double envelope house, 63; gangnail house, 83; Northbay house, 34, 36; open plan house, 50; portable heaters, 96; solarium house, 69; VPS house, 40

Baer, Steve, 93

Bathrooms: gangnail house, 80; manufactured core, 101; Northbay house, 26; open plan house, 50

Bay window: open plan house, 47

Beadwall, 93

Benson, Richard, 25

Box, Richard, 114

Breadbox water heaters: double envelope house, 63; gangnail house, 80; Northbay house, 36; open plan house, 50

Brick as thermal mass, 32, 59, 80

British thermal units (Btus), 32, 54

Building a home, 102

Building code: exceptions, 35, 56, 75, 80

Buying a house: economic attitudes, 20; reasons, 18

C

Chimney effect, 34

Clerestories, 89, 91; used with reflectors, 93

Climate: guiding factor in design, 93; regional designs for coping, 15

Closers in passive-solar designs, 93

Clustering of housing units, 20, 85, 115

Concrete: floor, finishing, 38; piers, 59; precast, 96; structures, water-filled, as thermal mass, 91; as thermal mass, 32, 68

Condominiums, 104

Conduction, 31; flat-plate collectors, 41; heating open plan house, 48

Construction industry: effect of small houses, 107

Contest. See Affordable Housing Competition

Continuous perimeter foundation, 38, 58

Convection, 31, 92; flat-plate collectors, 41; moving heated air, 58; moving heated water, 53

Cooling, 92, 94; double envelope house, 57, 64; evaporative methods, 95; gangnail house, 83; manufactured core, 101; mechanical devices, 14; open plan house, 55; passive-solar systems, 14; roof ponds, 92; solarium house, 74; use of overhangs, 30; VPS house, 44

Cool Pool, 92

Crawl space: double envelope house, 58, 64; open plan house, 48

D

Davis, Phil, 25

Degree-days, 30

Design specifications: double envelope house, 58; gangnail house, 78; Northbay house, 26; open plan house, 48; solarium house, 68; VPS house, 38

Dining area: gangnail house, 80; open plan house, 47; VPS house, 40

Direct gain, 33, 59, 80; distributing sunlight, 91; shading devices, 91; thermal mass needed, 34, 91

Domes, 98, 99

Double envelope house, 57-65, 103

About the Author

Dan Hibshman is a writer and editor who specializes in writing about the quality of life in nonurban areas. Born in Cleveland, Ohio, in 1945, he is a former elementary school teacher and has experienced the challenges of developing a self-sufficient lifestyle in rural northern California. Currently he teaches writing at a community college and edits a small regional magazine. He lives with his wife and two children in Willits, Mendocino County, California.